Sharks

Sharks

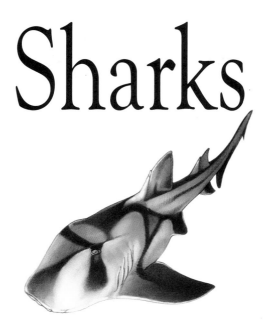

CONSULTANT EDITOR
Terence I. Walker

FOG CITY PRESS

Published by Fog City Press
814 Montgomery Street
San Francisco, CA 94133 USA

Copyright © 2002 Weldon Owen Pty Ltd

WELDON OWEN PTY LTD
Chief Executive Officer John Owen
President Terry Newell
Publisher Lynn Humphries
Managing Editor Janine Flew
Art Director Kylie Mulquin
Editorial Coordinator Tracey Gibson
Editorial Assistants Marney Richardson, Kiren Thandi
Production Manager Martha Malic-Chavez
Business Manager Emily Jahn
Vice President International Sales Stuart Laurence
European Sales Director Vanessa Mori

LIMELIGHT PRESS PTY LTD
Project Management Helen Bateman
Project Editor Klay Lamprell
Designer Emma Sutton
Consultant Editor Terence I. Walker

ISBN 1 876778 80 6

Color reproduction by Colourscan Co Pte Ltd
Printed by LeeFung-Asco Printers
Printed in China

A Weldon Owen Production

Welcome to the
Home Reference Library

We have created this exciting new series of books with the help of an international team of consultants, writers, editors, photographers, and illustrators, all of whom share our common vision—the desire to convey our passion and enthusiasm for the natural world through books that are enjoyable to read, authoritative as a source of reference, and fun to collect.

Finding out about things *should* be fun. That's the basic premise of the *Home Reference Library*. So, we've ensured that every picture tells a story, every caption encapsulates a fascinating fact, and every paragraph contains useful or interesting information.

It is said that seeing is believing. We believe seeing is understanding, too. That's why in the *Home Reference Library* we have combined text and images in an imaginative, dynamic design style that conveys the excitement of finding out about the natural world. Cut-away cross-sections detail the inner workings of a termite mound or the 2,000-million-year-old rock strata of the Grand Canyon. Photographs reveal extraordinary facts about the minutest forms of animal life, aspects of the behavior of nature's fiercest predators, or the beauty of a world far beyond our planet.

Each handy-sized book is a complete source of reference on its subject. Collect all the titles in the *Home Reference Library* series to compile an invaluable encyclopedic resource that you'll return to again and again.

From the editors of the *Home Reference Library*.

There is, one knows not what sweet mystery about this sea, whose gently awful stirrings seem to speak of some hidden soul beneath.

Moby Dick
Herman Melville (1819–91), American novelist

Contents

SHARK SHOWCASE 164

SHARK ESSENTIALS

Evolution and definition.
The world of water.
Biology and behavior.

The Basics

SHARKS ARE FISHES that have evolved over the past
450 million years to become dominant in the oceans of
the world. Their closest relatives—rays, skates, and the
strange-looking chimaeras—share their basic features,
though none has equaled the superb adaptations that make
sharks one of the most successful group of species on Earth.

FISH FEATURES

Sharks share most of the major internal and external features of their finned relatives, and make up about 1 percent of all fishes. Like all fishes, sharks use gills to extract oxygen from the water in which they live. The body of most species has three types of unpaired fins (dorsal, anal, and caudal, which is the tail fin) and two sets of paired fins (pelvic and pectoral). Swimming is achieved by side-to-side undulations of the body and tail, which create forward propulsion.

INTERNAL DIFFERENCES

One of the main internal features that set sharks apart from other fishes is that their skeletons, while strong and sturdy, are made of cartilage—a light, flexible, durable substance—instead of bone. This is why sharks are known as cartilaginous fishes. **Flotation aids** Unlike fishes, sharks do not have an internal swim bladder to help achieve neutral buoyancy, but instead rely upon their low-density cartilage, hydrodynamic planing, and liver

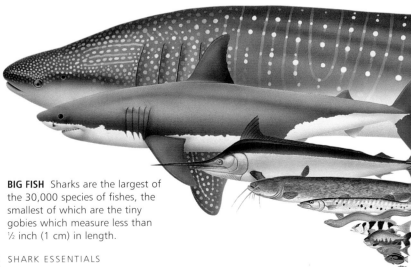

BIG FISH Sharks are the largest of the 30,000 species of fishes, the smallest of which are the tiny gobies which measure less than ½ inch (1 cm) in length.

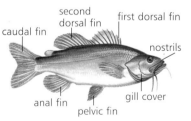

STANDARD DESIGN Though there is an impressive range of sizes, shapes, and color patterns of fishes, all fishes—including sharks—are built on the same basic body plan. Compare these two illustrations. Sharks, however, have some special adaptations for predatory, hydrodynamic efficiency.

caudal fin
second dorsal fin
first dorsal fin
nostrils
anal fin
pelvic fin
gill cover

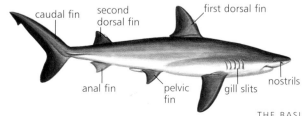

caudal fin
second dorsal fin
first dorsal fin
anal fin
pelvic fin
gill slits
nostrils

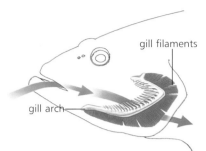

gill filaments

gill arch

GILLS IN ACTION All fishes breathe by taking in water through the mouth—and spiracle in some species—and forcing it out through gill slits. In sharks, unlike most other kinds of fishes, the gill slits can be seen.

oils to keep from sinking. Since oil, or squalene, is lighter than water, the liver acts as a float.

Slack jaw Some of the most notable differences in the anatomy of sharks and most bony fishes are found in the construction of the jaw, the method of its suspension from the head, and the organization of the teeth. In most sharks, the upper jaw is seated on the underside of the skull where it is loosely attached by ligaments and connective tissue. It is suspended from the

skull by cartilage, which attaches near the back corner of the jaw. This permits the upper jaw to be thrust out from the skull during feeding, allowing some species of shark to take large, powerful bites from relatively large prey.

Sense and sensibility All fishes find prey using an amazingly wide range of senses, which include chemoreception. Sharks have a highly developed ability to detect water vibrations through the sensory cells along their lateral line, and a sophisticated electrosensory system, localized in specialized sense organs on their head and jaw.

electroreceptors

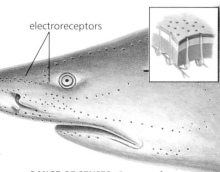

RANGE OF SENSES Groups of modified pores on sharks' heads are linked to sensory cells in jelly-filled tubes known as ampullae of Lorenzini.

TYPES OF SCALES Of the four types of fish scales shown right, the toothlike, or placoid scales, are characteristic of sharks.

EXTERNAL DIFFERENCES

All of the shark's five to seven gill slits are visible, while the gills of most other fishes are protected by a bony plate known as a gill cover or operculum. The shark's fins are thick and relatively stiff, and lack the delicate bony spines that are found in the fins of most bony fishes.

Scaly creatures The shark's skin has a layer of tiny, tough, dermal denticles, or scales, as opposed to the much larger flattened scales in most other fishes. These placoid scales allow water to flow smoothly over the body, reducing drag. As a result, sharks can cruise at 3 miles per hour (5 km/h), and the fastest sharks, such as the mako, are capable of bursts of up to 22 miles per hour (35 km/h). In the illustrations to the right, the part of the scale that is embedded in the skin of the fish is represented by the orange coloring.

Clenoid

Cycloid

Ganoid

Placoid

THE TYPICAL SHARK

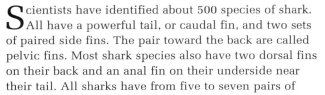

Scientists have identified about 500 species of shark. All have a powerful tail, or caudal fin, and two sets of paired side fins. The pair toward the back are called pelvic fins. Most shark species also have two dorsal fins on their back and an anal fin on their underside near their tail. All sharks have from five to seven pairs of gill openings and gills, which absorb oxygen from the water. All sharks are meat-eaters. Their food ranges from tiny plankton to large dolphins.

Bonnethead
Active coastal swimmer

SMALLEST & LARGEST

Sharks vary greatly in looks and in size. The smallest shark, the dwarf lantern shark, can fit into the palm of your hand. It grows to only 8 inches (20 cm) long.

The biggest shark is the whale shark. It can grow to 39 feet (12 m).

Tasselled wobbegong
Small, flattened bottom-dweller

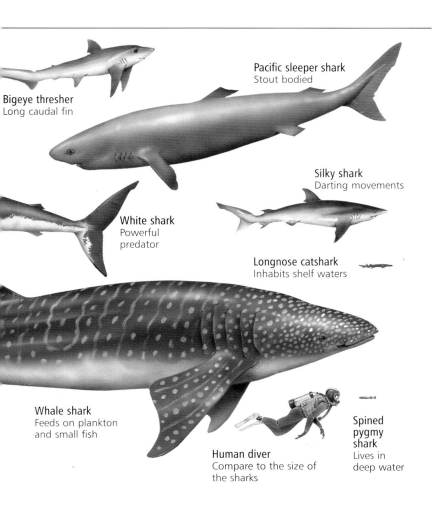

Bigeye thresher
Long caudal fin

Pacific sleeper shark
Stout bodied

Silky shark
Darting movements

White shark
Powerful
predator

Longnose catshark
Inhabits shelf waters

Whale shark
Feeds on plankton
and small fish

Human diver
Compare to the size of
the sharks

**Spined
pygmy
shark**
Lives in
deep water

CLOSE RELATIVES

Closely related to sharks, rays and skates (collectively known as batoid elasmobranchs) are represented globally by more than 700 species. They are widespread in almost all bottom-dwelling communities of the oceans, inhabit offshore environments, and extend into many inland freshwater habitats. Batoids made a relatively recent appearance in evolutionary history, some 200 million years after the first sharks.

so taxonomists must examine several specimens to distinguish features of a species. Additionally, unknown species may lurk in the ocean depths.

HARD TO IDENTIFY
Rays are among the most distinctive of the cartilaginous fishes but their classification is difficult and the subject of ongoing scientific debate. Males and females and the young can differ vastly in shape and color,

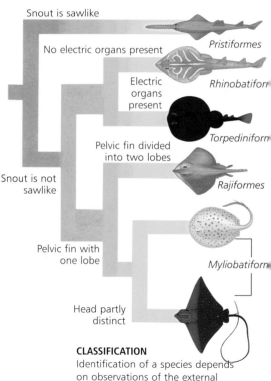

Snout is sawlike

No electric organs present

Pristiformes

Electric organs present

Rhinobatifor...

Torpediniform...

Pelvic fin divided into two lobes

Snout is not sawlike

Rajiformes

Pelvic fin with one lobe

Myliobatiform...

Head partly distinct

CLASSIFICATION
Identification of a species depends on observations of the external features of more than one specimen.

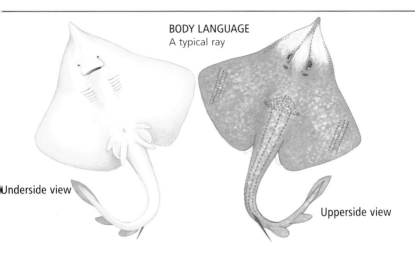

BODY LANGUAGE
A typical ray

Underside view

Upperside view

SEPARATING FEATURES

Living rays and skates have some important features that separate them from the sharks. The main body is highly flattened, both on the bottom and on top. Unlike most sharks, which have short and stout pectoral fins that extend from the body below and behind the head, the pectoral fins of the batoids are attached at the back of the skull, and are greatly enlarged to form a body disk. Some batoids, such as guitarfishes, skates, and electric rays, have well-developed dorsal and caudal fins, and strong tails. Others, such as stingrays, eagle rays, and devilrays, have greatly reduced tails that usually have only a rudimentary caudal fin, if any. Generally, the tail of most rays is usually reduced in size and not used for swimming. Instead, locomotion comes from the undulation of the tips of the pectoral fins. The majority of species either lack dorsal and caudal fins on the tail, or have small ones.

Getting defensive Many batoids, such as whiptail stingrays, stingarees, eagle rays, and some devilrays, have sharp spines on the tail. These venomous weapons are used defensively against large shark predators and also during social interactions among their own species.

Breathing equipment A major difference between sharks and rays is the positioning of the gill slits. In batoids they are located on the bottom surface of the body, whereas in sharks they are found along the sides. Like several bottom-dwelling sharks, the batoids have well-developed spiracles behind the eyes, and these serve to take in water for breathing when the ray is at rest

IN CLOSE-UP
The enormous Atlantic torpedo ray has a well-developed mouth and nostrils.

on the bottom or the mouth is being used for feeding.

The senses The eyes, positioned on top of the body rather than on the sides, provide a good view of the bottom around the animal, the distant horizon, and the waters above, but batoids are blind to their lower surface. Objects, such as prey items, under the animal

DIVERSITY IN SIZE Batoid fishes show a wide range of body forms and sizes, from small, bottom-dwelling stingarees that may be only the size of a human hand, to the massive manta rays (left) and spotted eagle rays (top right) that swim in the open ocean..

are detected and located by a well-developed olfactory system in front of the mouth, and lateral line and electroreceptor systems that span much of the body's underside.

Sizeable brains Though the brain of a ray is small and simple compared with that of a dolphin or seal, in ratio to body weight it is surprisingly large. This ratio is similar to that found in birds and marsupials. Of the cartilaginous fishes, rays have the biggest brains, with the manta ray having the largest of all.

FOOD FANCIES

All rays are carnivorous but most occupy a level below that of sharks in the food chain hierarchy. Whereas sharks are important predators on reefs and in open water, rays play a more significant role as predators on soft substrates. Large rays, including several torpedo rays, stingrays, and skates, are known to feed on fishes. However, small mobile invertebrates, such as sand worms, crustaceans, and mollusks, are more important dietary items.

MORE CLOSE RELATIVES

The closest living relatives of the sharks and rays are the chimaeras, which are thought to be descended from the same direct evolutionary lineage. Chimaeras, sharks, skates, and rays are within the same taxonomic class, Chondrichthyes. There are approximately 50 species of chimaeras globally. Their ghostly appearance and unique body form have given rise to a wide array of common names, including spookfishes, ghost sharks, ratfishes, and elephant fishes. Most live near the bottom on the continental shelf, and on the continental slope.

BODY TYPES

All chimaeras have rather elongate, soft, scaleless bodies with a bulky head covered in prominent sensory canals, a single gill opening, a prominent spine before the first dorsal fin, and only three pairs of large, often beak-like, teeth in the mouth. Water for breathing is taken in through the large nostrils rather than the mouth. The snout is highly modified in some of the genera. The elephant fish, for example, uses its hoe-shaped snout to probe the substrate for invertebrates, such as mollusks, on which it feeds. The snouts of

NAME GAMES Although its scientific name means water rabbit, the other common name of the blunt-nose chimaera is spotted ratfish, because of its long, tapering tail.

LONG HISTORY The harmless, silvery relatives of sharks and rays, like this elephant fish, look much like the extinct relatives from which they evolved about 340 million years ago.

spookfishes are extended to form a conical or paddle-shaped appendage, used for sensory perception. In addition to the claspers typical of sharks and rays (reproductive organs on the ventral fin used for transmitting seminal fluids), male chimaeras have retractable sexual appendages before the pelvic fins and on the forehead. These spiny structures are used to clasp the female during copulation.

SIZE COMPARISON Chimaeras are small to moderate in size, attaining 5 feet (1.5 m), excluding the fleshy filament that is sometimes present at the tail tip.

IN THE BEGINNING

The fossil record of sharks extends back through Earth's history more than a hundred times as far as that of humans and is three times as long as that of the dinosaurs. In total, the history of the development of sharks represents more than 450 million years of independent evolution.

STONE BONES

Pieces of internal skeleton and complete fossil sharks have rarely been discovered because cartilage is too soft to fossilize easily. The most numerous fossils of sharks are their teeth. Over the span of just a few years, a shark may grow, utilize, and then discard tens of thousands of teeth, making shark teeth probably the world's most common vertebrate fossils. Virtually every paleontologist has found fossil shark teeth.

Early finds The earliest sharklike fossils have been found in rocks that formed in the Devonian period of Earth's geological formation. The shark species we

SHARKS IN TIME Earth's geological history is divided into eras and periods. The earliest sharklike fossils are found in rocks that formed in the Devonian period.

Precambrian Time	Cambrian	Ordovician	Silurian	Devonian
				Paleozoic
4,600 million years ago	550	505	435	408	360

Stage 1

Stage 2

Stage 3

Stage 4

FACES IN THE DUST Transformed over millions of years to stone, the bones and teeth of ancient creatures are gradually revealed by the slow movements of the surrounding terrain and the effects of erosion.

LONG EXTINCT Among the most ancient and primitive sharks is *Cladoselache*.

see today appeared some millions of years later, in the Cenozoic era, though *Cladoselache*, which is about 375 million years old, shares many characteristics with modern sharks. Its tail (caudal fin) was similar in shape to those of the fast-swimming mako and white sharks. Some specimens contain whole fishes swallowed tail first, which suggest it had great speed and agility, a characteristic that no doubt helped it avoid being eaten by the giant armored fishes (placoderms) that shared the oceans with it.

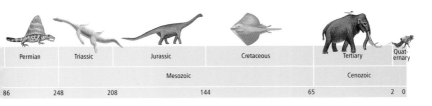

Permian	Triassic	Jurassic	Cretaceous	Tertiary	Quaternary
		Mesozoic		Cenozoic	
86	248	208	144	65	2 0

Other discoveries We are only just beginning to understand the diversity achieved by other Paleozoic sharks. Discoveries in the United States, Europe, and Australia reveal that some were armored by blade-like spines projecting from the dorsal fins. In others, only the males possessed these structures, which sometimes curved grotesquely over the head. Yet others had great spirals of serrated teeth, like slowly growing circular-saw blades, wedged under the chin. Around 350 million years ago, some sharks began evolving into bizarre creatures from which the living chimaeras are descended.

Slow motion Following this great period of shark radiation there seems to have been prolonged evolutionary slowing. From about 300 to 150 million years ago most fossil sharks can be assigned to just two groups. One of these (called xenacanths) was almost exclusively confined to freshwater environments. In spite of this, between its origin (about 450 million years ago) and its extinction (about 220 million years ago) it achieved global distribution.

The other group (called hybodonts) appeared some 320 million years ago and was predominant in oceans and freshwater habitats throughout the age of dinosaurs, particularly during the Triassic and Jurassic periods. The hybodonts were gradually ousted by modern forms toward the end of that era and finally became extinct at the same time as the last dinosaurs.

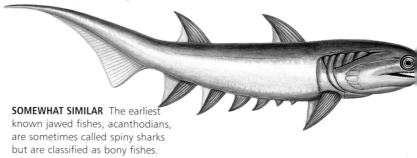

SOMEWHAT SIMILAR The earliest known jawed fishes, acanthodians, are sometimes called spiny sharks but are classified as bony fishes.

THE MODERN PERIOD

The earliest geological records of modern sharks are represented in fossil mako and mackerel shark teeth from about 100 million years ago. Teeth of primitive carcharhinids are recorded soon after. The oldest white shark teeth date from 60 to 65 million years ago.

Early in white shark evolution there are at least two lineages: one with coarsely serrated teeth that probably gave rise to the modern great whites, and another with finely serrated teeth and a tendency to attain a gigantic size. This group reached maximum development globally about 10 to 25 million years ago and includes the gargantuan *Carcharodon megalodon*. It may

OLD AND NEW Living sharks, like the fast-swimming mako, have changed very little in basic form in the past 60 million years.

be significant that the first appearance of large predatory sharks coincides with the extinction of dinosaurs and the widespread diversification of mammals. Some early mammalian groups evolved into aquatic forms around that time and wherever there are fossil teeth of the big sharks, there is also an abundance of marine animal bones with signs of having been chewed by sharks. It may be that modern shark evolution is linked with the rise of marine mammals, some 60 million years ago.

ADAPTATION RULES

As can be seen by the geological time scale they have spanned, sharks have been exceptionally successful. Their success is due essentially to the body design they inherited from their primitive ancestors, but sharks also demonstrate some fascinating adaptations to a variety of ecological niches. These adaptations have enabled them to become a dominant group, and the most important predators, in the sea.

WAY OF LIFE

A shark's body form is closely related to its way of life. The requiem family, which includes the blue shark, probably provides the classic features considered to epitomize a typical shark: a streamlined body, longish snout and pectoral fins, a tail fin with the upper lobe longer than the lower lobe, and a thickish caudal tail stem. This design provides for a highly efficient and graceful system of movement suited to their widespread distribution and broad spectrum of prey.

Power swimmers Mackerel sharks, such as the mako and the great white, are conico-cylindrical and more stout than the requiem sharks, making them less graceful but faster and more powerful. Their somewhat stiff, tuna-like body form is specialized for delivering bursts of high cruising

SLUGGISH TYPES Bottom-dwellers, like the necklace shark, have an eel-like appearance indicative of their less active lifestyle and their diet of the invertebrates and small fish found on shallow, rocky reefs.

speeds or for cruising
at relatively low speeds for long
periods of time.

Slow movers Not all sharks
require a high degree of hydrodynamic efficiency for their
survival. Sharks that lead a
sluggish existence, feeding near
or on the bottom in shallow
water, are characterized by a large
head, tapering body, and thin,
weak tail. The carpetsharks and
catsharks, including angelsharks
and necklace sharks, swim with a
pronounced eel-like motion, with
the motive force provided by the
whole rear end of the body, not
just the tail.

DIET RULES

Sharks are carnivores, occupying
nearly all feeding levels of marine
food webs. Among the range of
species, there are many adaptations for feeding. While sharks
do not chew, species such as the
hornsharks and bonnethead
sharks, which consume armored
invertebrates, have small, sharp
teeth at the front of the jaw for
grasping their prey and flat,

Blue shark

Great white

Hornshark

Shortfin mako

molariform teeth at the back to
crush the hard shell before
swallowing. Requiem sharks,
such as the blue shark, have
triangular teeth with serrated
edges to cut large fish and
cephalopods into pieces before
swallowing. This tooth design
reaches its climax with the large,
triangular, and serrated teeth of
the great white shark. Other
species, such as the shortfin
mako, have long, thin, needle-like
teeth for sinking into and
grasping large fish.

Camouflage

■ Camouflage, a combination of instinct and anatomy, is an adaptation that allows the shark to defend itself and to capture its prey more easily. Some sharks will utilize behavioral methods of camouflaging themselves. Nurse sharks, for example, will curl their pectoral fins under to form a dark, cave-like area in the water. Fish seeking refuge from predators swim in and are ambushed. Other sharks have natural camouflage in the form of coloration and body markings.

TRICKS OF THE TRADE

Natural camouflage is sometimes found only in young sharks, when they are most vulnerable to predation. This is true of species such as tiger sharks, zebra sharks, gray carpetsharks, and whiskery sharks, which have vivid stripes or blotches that eventually fade as they mature.

Deadly disguise In-shore, bottom dwelling sharks whose homes are rough seabeds often have mottled spotted color patterns that blend in with rocks, reefs, or marine plants. A prime example is the wobbegong, a type of carpet shark. It is an aggressive feeder that is superbly camouflaged in its reef habitat because of its mottled skin and the weed-like tassels that surround its mouth.

Illusionary tactics Sharks that spend most, or all, of their lives

BLENDING IN The patterning of the slow-moving leopard shark makes it difficult to see in areas where light dapples through floating kelp and shadows abound.

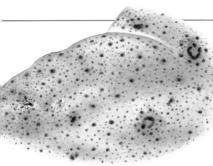

HIDE AWAY Angelsharks spend much of their day buried in the sandy ocean floor.

swimming are often counter-shaded to reduce their visibility in the water. The underside is lightly colored so that when viewed from beneath, the sharks blend with the sunlit water. On the upperside these sharks are darker so that when viewed from above they are difficult to distinguish from the ocean. The mako shark, which operates most of its life in the open ocean, is vivid blue on its upper surface and sides and white underneath.

Double trouble Many sharks have a back-up defense system to support their camouflage capabilities. The hornshark, which has small dark spots on its body and fins and hides easily amongst rocks in shallow-water kelp beds, also has two sharp spines on its back. If a predator finds it, the hornshark wedges itself into the rocks so that only the "horns" face out. The patterned swellshark, which also camouflages well in rocky reefs, can inflate its stomach with water until it is so firmly stuck in a crevice, it cannot be pulled out.

ON THE SURFACE

The oceanic whitetip shark, as the name suggests, has conspicuous, mottled, white tips on its fins and the tip of its tail. These markings help disguise this aggressive shark when it comes to the surface of the open ocean where it lives.

Oddities

■ While there are physical characteristics common to every shark, few look alike. Extremes of body form are an adaptation developed, over long periods of time, in response to environment and availability of food.

Big heads One function of the bizarre head of the hammerhead sharks is to act as a "wing," providing extra lift at the front of the shark that enables it to bank quickly and make rapid vertical movements. The dorso-ventrally flattened head induces minimal drag during turning. Since the smooth hammerhead sharks and scalloped sharks feed extensively on squid, which are jet-propelled and extremely maneuverable, the "hammer" enables these sharks to catch their fast and agile prey. This adaptation has been taken beyond mere hydrodynamic considerations in the winghead shark, whose head is wider, relative to its body, than any other shark. The location of the eyes at the end of the "wings" gives them superior binocular vision.

Big mouths Since the three giants of the shark world, the whale

SUPER SENSITIVE The extended nasal area and additional electroreceptors in hammerheads increase their olfactory and bioelectrical sensitivity.

GENTLE GIANT The whale shark, the largest fish in the world, is harmless to humans. The 300 rows of tiny teeth on each jaw are used to capture plankton.

shark, the basking shark, and the megamouth shark, are filter-feeders, they must take in many gallons of water to get enough food. They use their massive mouths to scoop up a living soup of water, tiny plant and animal plankton, fish eggs, and small fish. They flush the water through their gill slits before swallowing the strained food.

NOSY TYPE

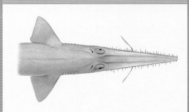

The unusual-looking longnose sawshark is a generally timid creature which uses its jagged snout to strike predators and prey. It trails the barbels on either side of its snout along the seabed to locate the small bony fish that it eats.

Water World

THE RANGE OF WATER MASSES in the world provide a rich and varied sensory environment for sharks. There are constant variations in temperature, concentration of chemicals, and ambient sound, light, and movement. Changes in bottom and coastal topography and fluctuations in Earth's magnetic field provide navigational obstacles and cues. At the same time, sharks must share this world with an abundance of other animals and plants, interacting with an endless procession of predators and prey.

SHARKS AT HOME

Sharks are superbly suited to the constantly changing environment that both nurtures and challenges them, and they occupy a wide range of habitats. They can be found in all Earth's oceans from the warm waters of the tropics to the frigid seas of the polar zones, from shallow coastal waters to the depths of the ocean floor. Some also spend periods of time in freshwater habitats. Distribution of particular species is largely explained in terms of water temperature and water depth.

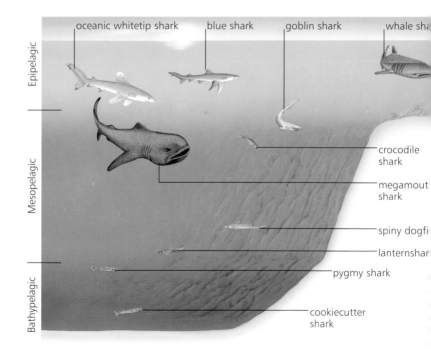

oceanic whitetip shark   blue shark   goblin shark   whale sha

Epipelagic

crocodile shark

megamout shark

Mesopelagic

spiny dogfi

lanternshar

pygmy shark

Bathypelagic

cookiecutter shark

COMMON HABITATS

Sharks are most varied in temperate and tropical seas, in the shelf waters of continents and islands, and on the adjacent deep-water slopes. There are fewer species in the sunlit upper reaches of the open ocean, very few in the deep ocean basins, and barely any at all in very deep water. Compared with the vast array of bony fishes, amphibians, reptiles, mammals, and birds that inhabit fresh water, sharks are represented in this environment by only a handful of species. And of these, only the bull shark is common and wide ranging, found in a variety of temperate and tropical freshwater habitats.

Bigger types Modern sharks are relatively large fishes, and they do not compete with bony fishes and invertebrates in habitats suitable for very small animals. There are no inshore shoals of small pelagic sharks, no tiny crevice or hole dwellers, no minute sharks with very small mouths that feed on invertebrates. Where sharks do thrive is in the role of moderate-sized to large marine predators. As such, whether they are benthic (bottom-dwellers) or active, they broadly overlap those habitats dominated by bony fishes and invertebrates, and feed extensively on the inhabitants of these micro-niches.

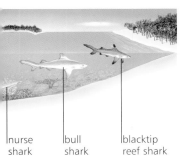

nurse shark

bull shark

blacktip reef shark

WATERY REALMS As well as the varying communities favored by sharks—coastal and inland, reef, or open ocean—three distinct oceanic depth levels are identified in this illustration. (These sharks are not drawn to scale.)

Freshwater

■ Very few species of shark venture far into a river system, mostly penetrating fresh waters only under the influence of tides, to breed. In general, sharks are not biologically suited to the highly variable conditions found in freshwater environments and are unable to compete ecologically with the many animals that thrive there.

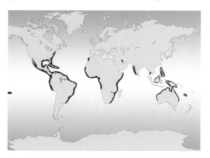

RIVER RESIDENT Widespread along continental coasts, the bull shark penetrates deeply into fresh waters.

PART-TIMERS

A number of shark species are considered marginal, occasionally penetrating brackish estuaries and the lower reaches of rivers with permanent sea access. Only two

Distribution map Bull shark

groups of large requiem shark occur in freshwater rivers and lakes far from the seas. Of these, the bull shark is the most successful, because it can tolerate highly salty sea water, as well as fresh water. It is often found in warm-temperate to tropical lakes and rivers, entering for periods of up to several weeks. The bull shark has been recorded as far as 1,750 miles (2,800 km) up the Mississippi River in the United States, and 2,500 miles (4,000 km) up the Amazon River in Peru. It has ample opportunity to encounter and attack people, which makes it more dangerous than great white or tiger sharks. **Rare types** River sharks are far less common, with only a few species in Asia and Australia,

some of which may be exclusive to freshwater rivers. The Ganges shark, once thought to be a bull shark because of its similar, stout appearance, is known only from the Ganges-Hooghly River system of the Indian subcontinent.

ENDANGERED SPECIES

Overfishing and degradation of the waters of the world by pollution is endangering sharks in freshwater habitats. These species are more vulnerable

FRESH LIVING Freshwater sharks are more threatened by pollution because the amount of fresh water in rivers and lakes is small compared with the amount of seawater on Earth.

because the amount of fresh water in rivers and lakes is comparatively small. They are vulnerable also because fresh water is mostly found in developing countries with large and expanding human populations and few controls.

Oceania

■ Sharks are primarily marine fishes. Many habitats are recognized in the world's oceans, with distinct boundaries for the different species of shark. Body form and way of life are related to a shark's location. Typifying the limited range of many smaller, active species of shark is the winghead shark, which is restricted to the Indo-Pacific region. Like many of the larger sharks, the tiger shark is an active swimmer, traveling vast distances each day and migrating according to seasonal changes. The whale shark, the largest of all sharks, also has one of the largest distributions.

COAST TO COAST

On a horizontal scale, habitats can essentially be distinguished as coastal and open water. Water temperature is an important factor in the diversity and distribution of sharks in coastal waters and in the upper reaches of the oceans. In some species, changes to coastal water temperatures bring about local and long-range migrations as sharks actively seek out waters within a suitable temperature range. Warm-water coastal and oceanic sharks often range into higher latitudes in summer and retreat toward the equator in winter, while cool-temperate species may

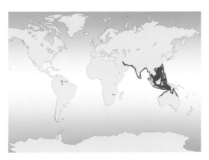

Distribution map Winghead shark

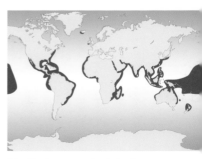

Distribution map Tiger shark

demonstrate the reverse pattern. Similarly, other coastal species may move between inshore and offshore waters in response to changing temperatures.

TOP TO BOTTOM

Some sharks are able to tolerate a wide range of depths, flourishing in both inshore and deep-water environments. The white shark primarily lives inshore but can also penetrate deep water on the continental slopes. The majority of deep-water shark species, however, are confined to deep water and have adapted specifically to this cold, inky environment.

BIG MOVERS To some extent, a shark's level of activity is determined by its size. Compare the attainable lengths of the sharks pictured (below) with the maps (below left) representing their different areas of distribution.

Whale shark 46 feet (14 m)

Tiger shark 24 feet (7.3 m)

Winghead 5 feet (1.5 m)

Distribution map Whale shark

Tropical

■ Sharks abound in the marine waters of coastal tropics where the water is usually warmer than 70°F (21°C). The Indo-West Pacific has the greatest number of shark species anywhere in the world. Sharks living in these regions include requiem sharks, hammerheads, many of the smooth houndsharks, wobbegongs, nurse and whale sharks, and some angelsharks. These can be further separated into active types which swim almost continuously, and bottom-dwelling (benthic) types, some of which move relatively little.

RESTRICTED RANGE Smaller tropical sharks operate in a limited area.

MOVERS AND SHAKERS

In winter, active tropical sharks will be closer to the equator, whereas in summer

Bonneth

they will be found much farther north or south, depending on the hemisphere in which they occur. Being such active swimmers and following seasonable water currents, many of the larger members of these species, such as the oceanic whitetip, are found in all the world's tropical waters. Smaller species of tropical marine sharks, less than 10 feet (3 m) long, tend to have smaller ranges. Examples are the spotted gully and bonnethead sharks.

Distribution map Spotted gully shark

Distribution map Bonnethead

FREE RANGING The oceanic whitetip shark occupies a free-ranging, predatory niche in tropical waters, dominating other shark species competing for food.

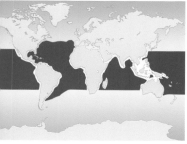

Distribution map Oceanic whitetip

Not so venturesome The bottom-dwelling tropical sharks also have relatively small ranges of distribution and are generally restricted to a particular archipelago or a region of the sea. These sharks spend most of their time on the ocean floor, waiting, camouflaged, to ambush their prey. Only the larger species, such as the nurse sharks and zebra sharks, will travel more than a few miles from their area in their lifetime.

Temperate

As with tropical sharks, temperate water sharks can be divided into active swimmers and bottom-dwellers. They live where water temperatures are between 50° and 70°F (10–21°C) and include species such as requiem sharks, hornsharks, smooth houndsharks, catsharks, mackerel sharks, thresher sharks and sand tiger sharks, some angelsharks, and the sawsharks.

BIG NOMAD The huge, filter-feeding basking shark tours cooler coastal areas, looking for plankton.

SEASONED TRAVELERS

The active swimmers follow water currents and temperature changes. In winter they tend to be closer to the equator and in summer they head away from it, going farther north, or farther south, than tropical sharks.

No-go zones Reflecting the pattern of tropical sharks, the larger species—more than 10 feet (3 m) long—are found virtually worldwide. However their preference for cooler waters means they have an antitropical distribution, meaning that while there are populations in both hemispheres, they are generally absent in tropical or equatorial seas. Included in this group are the basking and the great white.

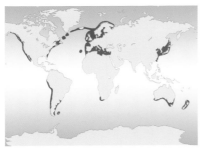

Distribution map Basking shark

Blurred boundaries When temperate sharks do venture into tropical waters, it is into the deeper, cooler areas. The blue shark, for example, is quite common near the surface in temperate areas and at depths of 200 feet (60 m) in the tropics. It is probably one of the widest traveling species. Other temperate sharks, such as the porbeagle shark and the salmon shark, will occasionally inhabit tropical waters but only within very exclusive ranges.

Like the smaller tropical species, small active temperate sharks—less than 6 feet (2 m) long—have more limited ranges than the larger species. However, like the larger forms, they have populations in both hemispheres and are generally absent from the tropics, with only a few venturing into cooler, deeper waters.

HOMEBODIES

Bottom-dwelling sharks in temperate waters, as in the tropics, are small, and because they move very little, their distribution is limited. So is their diet of herbivorous invertebrates and smaller fishes. Vast stands of kelp forests and sea-grass beds stretch along many temperate coastlines, providing rich food resources and effective shelter for these sharks.

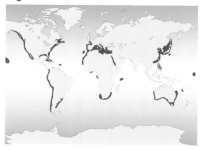

THE COOL TYPE The great white shark ranges widely, but stays away from the tropics.

Distribution map Great white shark

Cold Water

■ Temperature, more than latitudinal range is the important factor in considering the distribution of cold water sharks. Cool to cold water—colder than 50°F (10°C)—occurs at the surface in north and south temperate zones and in the Arctic and Antarctic oceans, but also at depth in temperate and even tropical seas.

GREENLAND SHARK This gigantic, sluggish dogfish has been recorded underneath polar ice floes.

BUSY BODIES

Since food is relatively scarce in cold waters, sharks that inhabit these waters, large and small, generally have to travel extensively to find enough appropriate prey. To allow this high level of activity, some sharks have structural adaptations, such as partial warm-bloodedness.

Large and small Large forms of active swimming cold water sharks, such as the Greenland shark and the salmon shark, can be found in the shallow waters of the far north and far south, especially during winter months.

In other, more temperate, areas they are found at depths in which the water temperature is almost the same as that of Arctic or Antarctic waters.

The small species of active cold water sharks—which are less than 3 feet (1 m) long—all live in depths of 1,000 feet (300 m) or more. They are not known to come close to the surface.

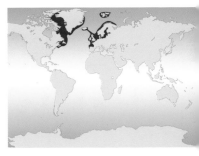

Distribution map Greenland shark

DWELLING DOWNUNDER

The bottom-dwelling cold sharks, too, are found only in deep, cold waters and never come close to the surface, even in the far north or the far south. Most are the size of the small, active, cold water sharks, but with a much more limited distribution. No light ever reaches these depths, so there are no plants. In some places, however, volcanic activity has created hot water vents where a host of sea creatures, such as mussels, clams, and huge tubeworms, thrive on bacteria, providing a source of food for the bottom-dwelling sharks that inhabit these waters.

SALMON SHARK A heavy, torpedo-shaped predator, this shark inhabits the more frigid waters of the North Pacific, from the surface to depths of 500 feet (155 m), and will rarely come close to shore.

Distribution map Salmon shark

PORBEAGLE The salmon shark and porbeagle were not recognized as two separate species until 1947, when it became understood that the porbeagle inhabits the North Atlantic.

Pacific Reef

Most islands and coral atolls in the central Pacific have a similar submarine reef profile. There is usually a shallow reef flat that separates the seaward reef from shallow backwaters or a large lagoon. The reef flat is often exposed at low tide, and is frequented by large fish only when flooded. These reefs provide food and shelter for a riot of plant and animal life, including many types of sharks. The specie composition and distribution of sharks on different Pacific reefs are remarkably similar.

NEAR AND FAR

Juvenile and adult blacktip reef sharks, common visitors to the reef flat during flood tide, frequent waters so shallow that their dorsal fins are completely exposed above the surface. They

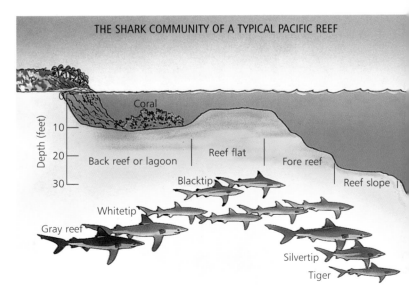

THE SHARK COMMUNITY OF A TYPICAL PACIFIC REEF

Coral

Depth (feet)

10

20

30

Back reef or lagoon

Reef flat

Fore reef

Reef slope

Blacktip

Whitetip

Gray reef

Silvertip

Tiger

...re an active species, capable of quick and rapid turns, and often move about the reefs in large groups, exhibiting high levels of excitement when feeding.

Getting deeper The shark most familiar to divers in the deep waters of central Pacific reefs is the gray reef shark. Very large groups of these sharks are reported in deep passes and channels that transect fringing reefs. They are best known for their threat display and can be aggressive without provocation.

AVOIDING COMPETITION To survive as one of many species in a specific habitat, sharks will generally develop different feeding habits and tastes.

Getting bigger The largest shark on most Pacific reefs is the tiger shark, a voracious predator with a wide diet that includes large stingrays and other sharks. It usually occurs in deep water on the seaward side of the reef flats, but also frequents deep channels and passes. Individuals will enter shallow water to feed on seabirds at rest on the water surface.

Deep Waters

■ Below and beyond the shallow reefs, but above the abyss, lies the layer of ocean called the deep mid-waters. From depths of about 650 feet (200 m), sea water is so dense that sunlight is filtered out.

Cookiecutter This tiny shark glow luminous green to attract pre

SURVIVAL TACTICS

Like other marine creatures that inhabit these regions, sharks of the deep mid-waters have two options for survival. Either they depend on dead and decaying animals falling from above, or they venture to the surface to find prey. Many small sharks ascend at dusk and return at dawn, relying on their large, often luminescent eyes and good vision in low light to detect prey.

Tiny terror The cookiecutter shark, named because it takes an oval-shaped plug of tissue from its prey, stays hidden in deep mid-waters, at around 2,000 feet (600 m), by day. At night it swims to the surface, using its bioluminescent light organs which glow in the dark to attract prey such as swordfish, tuna, billfishes, dolphins, other sharks, and even whales. Although widespread, its distribution seems to be limited to areas of specific depth.

Extrasensory The goblin shark, often considered to be the most mysterious and bizarre of all the sharks, occurs near the bottom on continental and island shelves and slopes, at depths of about 3,900 feet (1,200 m). As an aid to

Distribution map Cookiecutter

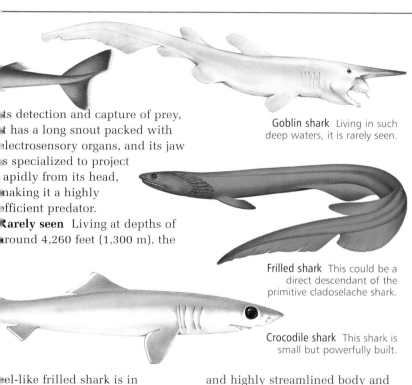

ts detection and capture of prey, it has a long snout packed with electrosensory organs, and its jaw is specialized to project rapidly from its head, making it a highly efficient predator.

Rarely seen Living at depths of around 4,260 feet (1,300 m), the

Goblin shark Living in such deep waters, it is rarely seen.

Frilled shark This could be a direct descendant of the primitive cladoselache shark.

Crocodile shark This shark is small but powerfully built.

eel-like frilled shark is in darkness most of its life. It is only occasionally seen on or near the surface in open waters. Its teeth are distinctive, and are probably used to grasp giant squid.

Mini torpedo Like the sand tiger shark to which it is related, the crocodile shark has a muscular

and highly streamlined body and is a fast-swimming predator. It grows to about 3 feet (90 cm) and lives at a depth of about 1,970 feet (600 m), chasing small prey near the surface at night. Widespread throughout the open oceans of the world, it feeds on shrimp, lanternfishes, and squid.

The Abyss

In the darkest depths of the ocean, more than 3,000 feet (1,000 m) below the surface, lies a strange and mysterious world. The water is very cold. It is pitch dark except for the light made by other animals, and the pressure can be a thousand times greater than at the surface. Although humans cannot dive this deep, scientists can travel down in submarines or deep-water submersibles and through the windows of these vehicles, they have been able to photograph and observe the inhabitants of this region, including the false catshark, the small spined pygmy

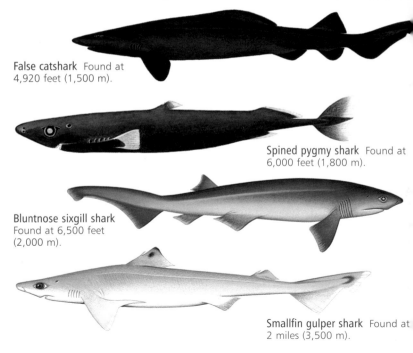

False catshark Found at 4,920 feet (1,500 m).

Spined pygmy shark Found at 6,000 feet (1,800 m).

Bluntnose sixgill shark Found at 6,500 feet (2,000 m).

Smallfin gulper shark Found at 2 miles (3,500 m).

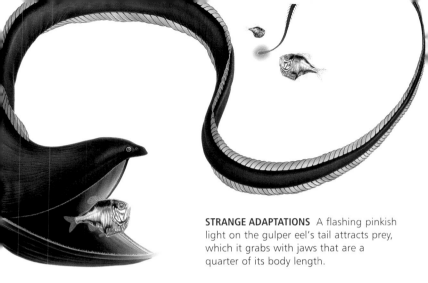

STRANGE ADAPTATIONS A flashing pinkish light on the gulper eel's tail attracts prey, which it grabs with jaws that are a quarter of its body length.

shark, the bluntnose sixgill, and tiny gulper sharks. Below 12,000 feet (3,660 m), scientists have observed shark relatives, such as the skate and chimaera, but have not found any sharks.

ADAPT OR DIE

Deep-sea creatures need adaptations that help them find and capture scarce food, avoid being eaten by desperate co-inhabitants, and seek out mates—in the dark. Many of these sharks are bioluminescent, producing their own light. The spined pygmy shark's belly is covered with tiny organs that produce just enough light to equal the faint glow that filters down from the surface when it swims to the upper waters to feed, helping it to camouflage itself from predators below.

Getting to the top Many deep-sea sharks have large livers (around 25 percent of their body weight) that contain up to 90 percent oil. The density of liver oil varies little with water depth, so these sharks can rise quickly toward the surface when chasing prey more easily than bony fish, which have gas bladders.

SHARKS UNDER GLASS

O n a global scale, there are approximately 100 species of shark on display. Not all species are suited to captivity, the major limitation being the size of the tank. The majority of sharks held in aquariums are sand tiger sharks, bull sharks, blacktip reef sharks, and whitetip reef sharks. However, with the increased size of modern aquarium tanks, better techniques in husbandry, and greater knowledge of shark biology, aquarists are increasingly able to display larger species in a more natural environment.

Injury-free collection Donation and breeding are the most common means of obtaining smaller sharks. The larger sharks tend to be more difficult to breed and harder to acquire through donation, so they are usually collected from the wild. This is a delicate operation. The shark is usually lassoed at sea, then constrained in a sling, sedated, and transported in a special tank.

IGGER AND BETTER As aquariums benefit from increased knowledge of sharks and dvanced technology, larger sharks, such as the whale shark (above) and the sand ger shark (left), can be safely accommodated.

Sharkworks

THE SHARK'S BODY IS BEAUTIFULLY attuned to life in an unforgiving watery world. Its form provides hydrodynamic efficiency and power, and signs relayed through a system of sophisticated sensory organs keep the shark fully informed about what is going on within and around it.

INSIDE OUTSIDE

M any features of the shark's body have evolved in response to the physical constraints of its dense aquatic environment. For example, its internal skeleton is composed of cartilage, an elastic tissue much higher in water content than bone. This allows a higher degree of body flexibility and agility, provides protection and support for organs, and reduces total body mass. It is unlikely that large, modern sharks would be capable of such quick, agile movement had they evolved bony skeletons.

TORPEDO-SHAPED

The benefits of a shark's cartilaginous skeletal system are commonly furthered by a fusiform (cigar-shaped) body. The snout and head are fused into a missile-like nose cone, and the diameter of the body is greatest at about a third of the way back from the snout, tapering off toward the tail. This shape lets water flow smoothly over the body, and reduces turbulence along the

spinal column

braincase

lower jaw

gill arch

pectoral girdle

FLEXIBLE BONES A shark's skeletal system is based on lightweight cartilage rather than heavy bone.

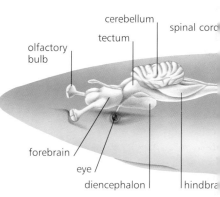

cerebellum

spinal cord

tectum

olfactory bulb

forebrain

eye

diencephalon

hindbrain

HEADY STUFF Sharks are intelligent enough to be capable of learning.

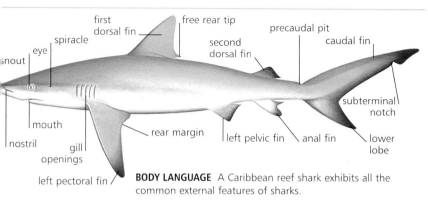

first dorsal fin
free rear tip
precaudal pit
caudal fin
spiracle
second dorsal fin
eye
snout
subterminal notch
mouth
rear margin
nostril
gill openings
left pelvic fin
anal fin
lower lobe
left pectoral fin

BODY LANGUAGE A Caribbean reef shark exhibits all the common external features of sharks.

kin. Swimming power and stability are provided by the shark's well-developed fins, including the caudal fin, or tail.

BRAIN POWER

Contrary to popular belief, shark brains are large in relation to their body weight out of water, and rival that of some birds and mammals. Like the brains of all vertebrate animals, the shark brain consists of hundreds of thousands of neuron cells which manage electrical impulses between the body and the brain. **Within the brain** The hindbrain processes information from many sensory systems, controls movements of the head and jaw, and interacts between the higher brain centers and the spinal cord. The cerebellum coordinates body movements. The tectum receives and integrates visual and other sensory information, while the diencephalon regulates hormone production and output. The forebrain receives information from the olfactory, electrosensory, and lateral line systems.

MUSCLE MIGHT

Sharks have two main types of muscles—red and white. Commonly, the red muscle lies in a thin layer just under the skin and outside the white muscle. It has a good blood supply and uses aerobic oxidation of fat as its energy source. Red muscle functions in sustained slow swimming and in a "typical" shark, such as a blue shark, comprises 11 percent of the total muscle. White muscle has a poor blood supply, functions by the anaerobic breakdown of glycogen and is used only during fast sprint swimming. Because white muscle operates anaerobically, sharks cannot sustain high sprint speeds and quickly become exhausted.

ORGAN ORGANIZATION

While a shark has essentially the same kinds of organs as other vertebrates, including those of humans, there are a few special adaptations. Of course a shark does not have lungs, but has gills so that it can breathe underwater.

Efficient digestion In order to manage the consumption of large marine animals, a shark's stomach can distend to fill a great part of the body cavity. The intestine is generally short, but its capacity to digest its food and absorb vital elements is greatly increased by a special spiral-shaped valve. The spiral shape enhances the efficiency of the digestive process by providing increased surface area of digestion, without an increase in the length of the organ.

Large liver A shark's liver is generally huge and extremely rich in oil. Being lighter than water, the oil in the liver helps to reduce the shark's overall density. This is important, as most sharks are negatively buoyant, meaning they are heavier than water and must expend energy in order to stop themselves from sinking. Their large, oil-rich liver acts as a float, in the absence of the air-filled swim bladder that enables most bony fishes to achieve buoyancy. The fatty oils in the liver also provide a store of energy so that some sharks can go for months without eating.

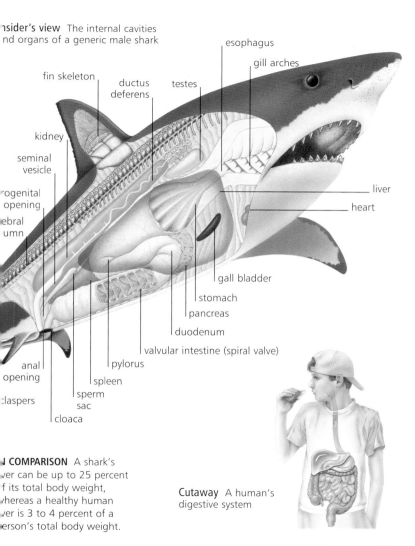

Insider's view The internal cavities and organs of a generic male shark

esophagus

gill arches

fin skeleton

ductus deferens

testes

kidney

seminal vesicle

urogenital opening

vertebral column

liver

heart

gall bladder

stomach

pancreas

duodenum

valvular intestine (spiral valve)

pylorus

anal opening

spleen

sperm sac

claspers

cloaca

COMPARISON A shark's liver can be up to 25 percent of its total body weight, whereas a healthy human liver is 3 to 4 percent of a person's total body weight.

Cutaway A human's digestive system

SHARK BREATH

A shark breathes by taking water into its mouth and, in many sedentary species, into paired spiracles behind its eyes. The water flows out over the gills which absorb oxygen for use in the shark's body, and deposit the carbon dioxide that is a waste product of metabolism. The oxygen that has been extracted is then transferred to the blood. **Blood-filled structures** Each gill has hundreds of feathery gill filaments that are filled with oxygen-absorbing blood, supplied by large arteries (which is why gills have a reddish color). Gill filaments are supported by a part of the shark's skeleton called the gill arches. The gills open to the outside through slits—usually five, sometimes six or seven. It is not known why some species have a greater number of gill slits but those that do are generally more primitive sharks.

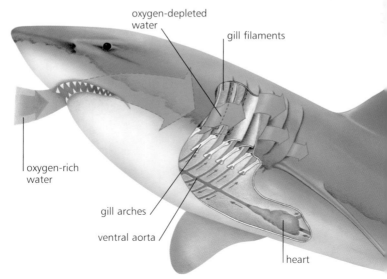

oxygen-depleted water

gill filaments

oxygen-rich water

gill arches

ventral aorta

heart

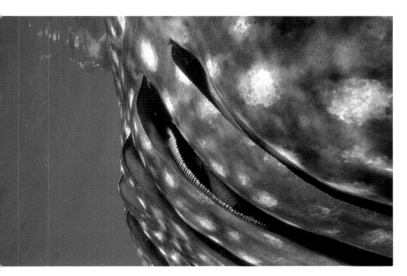

RAMMING IT IN

Some species—mainly sluggish bottom-dwelling forms such as catsharks and wobbegongs—pump water over their gills by rhythmically contracting muscles that open and close valves at the entrance and exit of the system.

Other species employ ram-jet ventilation, which uses the forward motion of the shark to move water backward over the gills. The highly active mackerel sharks, for example, rely entirely

FAST BREATHING Large, active sharks such as mako sharks and great whites need plenty of oxygen to utilize their muscle. Swimming fast forces larger volumes of oxygen-containing water over their gills.

on ram-jet ventilation and must keep swimming to breathe. Between these extremes, species such as the sand tiger and the piked dogfish are able to switch from respiratory pumping when at rest to ram-jet ventilation at cruising speeds, thereby saving energy useful for catching prey.

TALKING SENSE

All sharks are hunters—even the big filter-feeders. Since vision is limited underwater, sharks have developed a broad range of incredibly keen senses to aid them in locating prey, including at least one that is absent or poorly understood in most other animals.

A TYPICAL SCENARIO

Being attuned to the low-frequency sounds that travel through water, a shark can hear the sound of a boat anchoring on a coral reef miles away. When a person on that boat hooks a fish, tiny drops of the fish's blood filter into the water. The shark's sense of smell is so sharp that it can detect those few molecules of blood and will swim toward the scent. Pressure waves created while the shark swims bounce off obstacles, helping it to navigate quickly and accurately.

Nearing the boat, the shark can see flashes of the fish's silvery body as it struggles to free itself from the line. The closer it gets to the fish, the less the shark can see

it because its eyes are too far apart to see what is immediately in front of it. But the special electricity-sensitive pores on its snout aid the shark in detecting electrical impulses given off by the fish, allowing it to close in on its prey.

SPECIAL SENSES

The ability to detect the weak electrical fields created by a fish when it moves is provided by a network of jelly-filled pores, called ampullae of Lorenzini, which are spread across a shark's snout. This is a sense that humans don't have.

Two touchy A shark feels touch in two ways—through bodily contact and through sensing vibrations. Vibration-sensitive nerve cells, arranged in a series called the lateral line, run along a shark's sides and around its eyes and snout, helping a shark to "feel" objects several miles away.

SOMETHING EXTRA Hammerhead sharks, with their broad heads, have more ampullae of Lorenzini and can detect prey in sand and in crevices.

Sight and Hearing

Generally, vision is created when light enters an eye through the pupil, a lens focuses the light onto the nerve cells of the retina at the back of the eye, and the retina delivers information about that light to the brain.

Sharks have a special layer beneath the retina, a series of plates that function like mirrors, reflecting up to 90 percent of certain colors of light back into the light receptor cells of the eye. This increases the sensitivity of the eye. Many deep-sea sharks have big eyes to utilize this system to greatest advantage. Sharks that inhabit light, shallow waters can darken the plates with moveable pigments, much like pulling a curtain across a mirror.

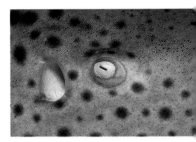

EAR APPARENT Pictured above are the eye and ear of a leopard shark.

BASIC VISION
Like many vertebrate, sharks have rigid eyeball enclosing light-sensitive receptor area the retina

WIDE VISION With eyes set on the ends of their "wings," hammerheads have tremendous side vision but must swing their head back and forth to see in front of them.

LISTEN HEAR

A shark's ears are visible as tiny openings in the top of its head. Its inner ears, called macula neglecta, are inside its braincase. The patches of hairlike cells that line the inner ears are stimulated by much lower frequency sound than humans can detect. Commonly, sharks are able to detect vibrations with frequencies below 1,000 hertz, or cycles per second. Some inshore sharks are able to detect sounds as low as 10 to 800 hertz. The range of vibrations humans can detect is generally much higher, from 25 to 16,000 hertz, with the most efficient hearing between 500 and 4,000 hertz.

In the balance The inner ears are also a shark's principal organ of balance and coordination. They regulate balance by detecting the motion of fluid within their cavities. They can also detect the pull of gravity, and changes in velocity and direction as the shark swims.

INNER EAR Sound enters through the endolymphatic pore to reach the inner ear.

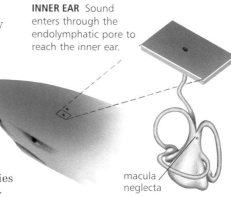

macula neglecta

NICTITATING EYE

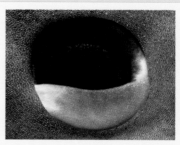

The eyes of most sharks are rimmed with immovable eyelids. However some have the lower lid folded into a nictitating membrane which closes over the eye during feeding and protects it from damage.

Smells and Tastes

Nerve cells in a shark's nose can detect one part blood in a million parts sea water. This ability to detect incredibly low concentrations of chemicals is derived through the nasal sacs inside their large nostrils. The sacs are lined with folded sensory tissues arranged in rows. As a shark swims, a fleshy flap across the center of each nasal sac channels water flow over the receptor-bearing olfactory tissue.

When sharks are at rest, the current created by means of respiratory pumping, whereby muscles rhythmically force water from the mouth to the gills, tends to draw a stream of water into the nostrils. Some bottom-dwelling sharks have nasal grooves

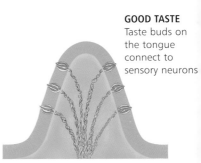

GOOD TASTE
Taste buds on the tongue connect to sensory neurons

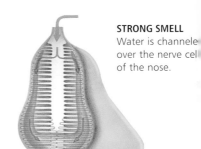

STRONG SMELL
Water is channeled over the nerve cells of the nose.

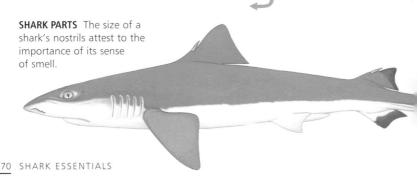

SHARK PARTS The size of a shark's nostrils attest to the importance of its sense of smell.

FINDING FAINT ODORS Port Jackson sharks hunt prey that hides in sand, so their noses have special folds that expose the maximum surface area to water.

connecting their nostrils to their mouths to further ensure that water manipulated by respiratory pumping also passes over the olfactory tissue.

TASTY TIDBITS

While the olfactory sacs on a shark's snout are the location of greatest chemical sensitivity, taste receptors on the roof and floor of the tongue and throat enable a shark to make a final discrimination of food before it is swallowed. Experiments suggest sharks have a well-developed ability to discriminate between tastes. Apart from its role in food selection, taste may also be involved in detecting differences in the salinity of water. A great deal of research is devoted to the way in which sharks respond to chemical stimuli through smell and taste, with the aim of creating an effective shark repellent.

Touch and ESP

■ Sharks can utilize extra-sensory perceptions that humans don't have or don't appear to have. Their ability to feel touch is offered a wider dimension by the lines of specialized hairlike cells that occur in pits, grooves, and canals along the shark's sides and in branches throughout the head. This is called the lateral line.

Good vibrations A shark that is swimming makes pressure waves that bounce off creatures and objects and return to the shark. The vibration-sensitive nerve cells of the lateral line detect the vibrations caused by the returning waves, discerning information about the direction of movement as well as the amount of movement. The importance of the lateral line is indicated by the large number of nerve fibers running between it and the brain—up to 6,000 sensory nerve fibers in some sharks.

ELECTRICAL CURRENTS

Sharks also have the ability to detect weak electrical voltages. Such electrical cues may emanate from prey animals or be produced by

EXTRA SENSORY The red line marks the position of most of the specialized hair cell receptors that are central to the shark's sensory system, known as the lateral line.

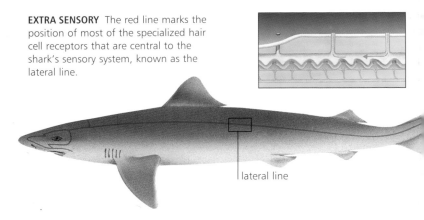

lateral line

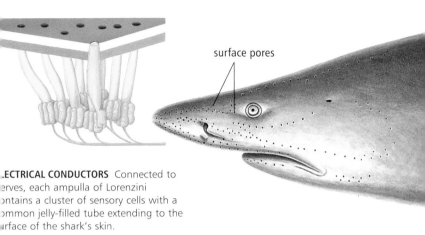

surface pores

ELECTRICAL CONDUCTORS Connected to nerves, each ampulla of Lorenzini contains a cluster of sensory cells with a common jelly-filled tube extending to the surface of the shark's skin.

currents flowing through Earth's magnetic field. Sharks may employ this "electrical sense" in ordinary daily orientation during long-distance migration. The sense organs involved in this electrical detection are the ampullae of Lorenzini—delicate jelly-filled canals connected to pores in the shark's snout. The pores form discrete patches on the head, distinct from the lateral line canals, and these can be very large and prominent in large, active pelagic sharks as well as in many deep-water sharks.

LATERAL THINKING

Vibrations enter through the shark's skin pores and stimulate the sensory hair cells, or neuromasts, which in turn stimulate an attached nerve fiber, which passes the "information" about the vibration to the shark's central nervous system.

TAILS

A shark's tail, or caudal fin, is its main means of propelling itself. As a shark swims, it bends its body from side to side; the tail bends more than the body and creates forward thrust.

TAIL TYPES

The shape of a shark's tail gives clues about how active it is. In all sharks, the spine extends through the tail to the tip of the upper lobe. Generally the upper lobe is epicercal (longer and heavier).

In the case of bottom-dwelling (benthic) sharks which feed on slow-moving prey such as shellfish, crustaceans, and other invertebrates, the vertebral column is nearly straight and the lower lobe is set low. They swim along the seabed in an eel-like manner, sweeping their tail slowly from side to side.

In active sharks, like tiger sharks which hunt fast-moving prey, the vertebral column is elevated into a crescent shape much like those of tuna and swordfishes.

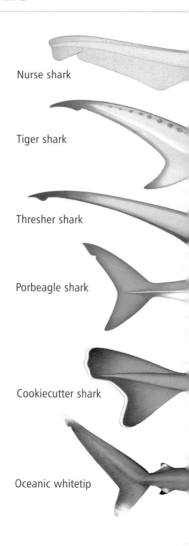

Nurse shark

Tiger shark

Thresher shark

Porbeagle shark

Cookiecutter shark

Oceanic whitetip

LETHAL WEAPON Thresher sharks use their long tails as a whip to herd together the small schooling fish they prey on.

Nurse sharks The nurse shark inhabits caves and crevices. Its prey consists of crabs, sea urchins, and octopuses. It uses sweeps of its elongated tail to propel it slowly in search of food.

Tiger sharks Their highly varied diet, which includes turtles, fishes, sea birds, stingrays, and other sharks, means that tigersharks must be able to cruise slowly, speed up quickly, and twist and turn rapidly. To achieve this kind of power, their tails are strongly epicercal.

Thresher sharks These have the longest tail of any shark. They are active hunters of fish and squid, which they herd, and then stun, with the powerful and incredibly elongated upper lobe of their tail.

Porbeagle sharks A voracious feeder on school fishes, the porbeagle's short, symmetrical tail is versatile, suited to slow cruising punctuated by sudden bursts of speed. Lateral "keels" at the base reduce drag.

Cookiecutter sharks The cookiecutter hunts squid and crustaceans, but will also attack large deep-sea fish and large sharks. Its tail, typical of active deep-water sharks, has broad lobes of almost the same size.

Oceanic whitetip sharks A large species usually found far offshore, the oceanic whitetip has a varied diet. It is generally slow-moving, but is capable of short bursts of speed due to the strength of its upper lobe.

FINS

Shark fins vary enormously between species, but all serve to help propel the shark and to adjust its movement. Some also provide camouflaging effects.

FUNCTION AND FORM

All species of shark have two sets of paired fins on the lower parts of their bodies—the pectoral fins near the front, and the pelvic fins toward the back. They also have between two and four unpaired fins, including the caudal fin (or tail), commonly two dorsal fins situated on the top of the body, and in most sharks, an anal fin which is usually the smallest of the fins. **Aerodynamic principles** Like aircraft wings, shark fins have streamlined cross-sections that are thick and rounded in front and tapering to a fine edge at the rear. In many sharks, the pectoral and pelvic fins are additionally convex on top and concave

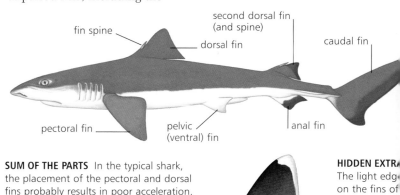

fin spine

second dorsal fin
(and spine)

dorsal fin

caudal fin

pectoral fin

pelvic
(ventral) fin

anal fin

SUM OF THE PARTS In the typical shark, the placement of the pectoral and dorsal fins probably results in poor acceleration, but the spacing between them is critical in interacting with the water flow to increase efficiency and thrust.

HIDDEN EXTRA
The light edge
on the fins of
silvertip shark
make its true
hard to gaug

elow, providing lift as the shark
moves forward.

Complete control The fins are
flexible and have internal
muscles that allow them to bend
and tilt while the shark is
maneuvering or braking. They
also generally have a rear notch
and a free rear tip that can be
moved sideways (in the case of
dorsal and anal fins) or up and
down (in the case of pectoral and
pelvic fins). By flexing their fins
to increase drag, sharks are able
to brake suddenly, allowing them
to stop and hover.

ADDED BENEFIT The spines
on a hornshark's dorsal fins
protect it from predators.

DIFFERENT VIEWS To humans, a shark's
fin in the surf means danger. To a shark
it means the ability to brake and turn,
accelerate and track, lift, and prevent
pitch, roll, and yaw.

JAWS

Shark jaws are simple but effective, consisting of a pair of upper and lower jaw cartilages. There is variety in shape and size depending on the shark's diet and method of feeding.

BETTER BITING

In the ancestral sharks, the mouth was at the front of the head rather than underslung, and the upper jaw was bound tightly to the cranium. The most important

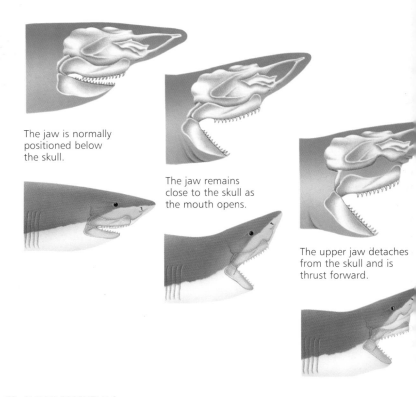

The jaw is normally positioned below the skull.

The jaw remains close to the skull as the mouth opens.

The upper jaw detaches from the skull and is thrust forward.

evelopment over time in the
esign of a shark was probably
ne freeing of the upper jaw from
ne cranium. In a modern shark,
ne upper jaw is loosely attached
o the skull by ligaments, small
uscles, and connective tissue.
is suspended from the skull by
ne hyoid cartilage, which
ttaches near the back of the jaw.

owerful bite This arrangement
ermits great mobility of the
ntire jaw mechanism. As the
hark lunges at its prey, the jaw
detaches from the skull and is
thrust forward. This protrusile
design is an important means of
increasing the power of a shark's
biting action, so that sharks such
as the great white are able to feed
on relatively large prey.

Body support This powerful
biting mechanism imposes
considerable forces on a shark's
body. To counteract this, the
dorsal and ventral processes have
been expanded to protect the
spine and to improve its stability.

TEETH

One unusual and highly successful feature of sharks is their teeth, which are continuously replaced through life. The teeth are not attached directly to the jaw cartilage but instead are embedded in a membrane called a tooth bed. Teeth are formed in a groove on the inside of the jaw cartilage and move progressively forward on the tooth bed. Eventually they erupt through the soft tissue overlying the replacement teeth to fold into place in the functional row. Because the bite is so powerful, teeth become blunt and are often broken. Frequent replacement overcomes this problem. A shark may go through mo[re] than 30,000 teeth i[n] its lifetime and ca[n] have up to 3,000 teeth in its mouth a[t] any one time.

Cookiecutter shark

Teeth of a gummy shark

Frilled shark

TAKES ALL TYPES The primitive shape of the frilled shark's teeth, the flat, woven-like patterns of the gummy shark's teeth and the serrated teeth of the cookiecutter shark demonstrate the variety to be found in sharks' teeth.

Goblin shark   Great white   Salmon shark   Upper and lower teeth

Megamouth

Tiger shark

Milk shark

SPECIALIZATION

Sharks usually have one kind of tooth, appropriate to what they eat. Mako sharks have stabbing teeth for grabbing fast prey. Wobbegongs have small, sharp teeth for crushing shellfish. Great whites have slicing teeth for cutting large prey into pieces.

Being unique Hornsharks are an exception. They have both grabbing and crushing teeth—perfect for grabbing and crunching into spiny sea urchins. This mixture of teeth is called heterodonty and it gives this order of sharks—the Heterodontiformes—its name.

Unusual types A primitive tooth type found in shark fossils is also found in modern frilled sharks. It has a single slender cusp, a number of smaller cusps either side of it, and a long flat base— excellent for grabbing fast, small fish. Cookiecutter sharks have large, highly specialized sawlike cutting teeth in their lower jaw. They suck onto their prey with their lips and swivel around, removing a plug of flesh. In this way, they can attack larger fishes. Gummy sharks appear to "gum" their prey, when in fact they have very flat teeth they use to crush bottom-dwelling creatures.

Skin Deep

Shark skin consists of dermal denticles (actually modified teeth), which give the skin its sandpaper texture. Though the roughness would seem to increase drag through friction, it is probable that the alignment of the denticles channels the water, resulting in a flow that acts to reduce friction. This arrangement also makes the sharks hydrodynamically quiet, a great advantage in stalking prey.

OLD AND NEW This close-up of a nurse shark's skin shows dark patches where old denticles have been shed.

VARIATIONS

Shark skin is tough and richly supplied with nerves, blood vessels, and sense organs. It consist of an outer layer (epidermis) with multiple layers of cells, and an inner layer (dermis) comprising cells in a network of fibers. The dermis is where the pigment occurs.

Different thicknesses In some deep-water lantern sharks the skin is thin and papery, whereas in whale sharks it can b more than 1 inch (2.5 cm) thick. Skin thickness may also vary withi species. Female blue sharks have much thicker skin on their back than the males, possibly to protect them during mating. In bottom-dwelling sharks the denticles are often large and rough, whereas in active sharks they are small, with parallel ridges on their crowns.

BLENDING IN Deep-water sharks are ofte dark brown or black, while inshore, bottom-dwelling sharks, like this nurse shark (right), are a mottled color.

Behaving
Themselves

SHARKS DEMONSTRATE behavior that often appears to us as erratic or dangerous, but which is, in fact, remarkably sophisticated and intelligent, driven by complex sensory systems. Far from being mindless, destructive automatons, sharks are capable of subtle social systems.

FEEDING

Sharks eat only what they need in order to survive, grow, and reproduce. They feed, on average, once or twice a week but some may go without food for months at a time.

TRACKING AND ATTACKING

As predators at the top of the food chain, sharks are highly proficient at detecting and tracking prey. Individual species may also have particular styles of hunting and attacking.

Food specialists Some sharks, such as the mako and great white outswim their prey. Others, such as the blue shark, tackle large schools of fish (pictured right), breaking up the mass and isolating smaller groups of the fish. Filter-feeders, such as the whale shark, swim with their massive mouths agape, scooping up their food. Bottom-dwellers, including the tasselled wobbegong, use their camouflage to take prey by surprise.

KEEN SENSES Sharks use many senses to find and capture prey. They are able to locate a fish over a long distance and can determine if it is healthy, wounded, dying, or dead.

Sensing dinner Sharks use their highly developed and complex sensory systems to find and capture their prey, and are able to detect healthy, wounded, dying, or dead fishes over long distances. Their acute olfactory and electrical senses are primary in most feeding situations. Healthy animals provide scent trails from mucus and the chemicals they emit. Odors from dead or bleeding animals travel many miles on ocean currents, and wounded fish also send out distinctive, low-frequency sounds that sharks can home in on. There is also some evidence to suggest that sharks can learn and remember where to find food. Since twilight and darkness are probably the most important times for a shark's feeding cycle, vision plays an important part only once a shark is within approximately 65 feet (20 m) of its prey. In the last split-seconds, touch and taste become critical.

ACTIVE EATERS Active hunting sharks feed mainly on bony fishes, cephalopods such as squid, and crustaceans such as lobsters (pictured right). Large, active sharks will also eat rays, turtles (pictured far right), dolphins, seals (pictured below), and even other sharks.

ON THE MENU

Sharks used to be thought of as the trash cans of the sea, consuming whatever they could find. While tiger sharks have been known to eat just about anything—including kangaroos and cows that have washed down flooded rivers, as well as plastic bags and cans of food—the majority of species are more discerning. Most have a varied diet to increase their chances of survival. Only a few have a highly specialized diet, such as the California hornshark, which feeds

BITE AND SPIT Particularly useful for killing prey with hard shells, such as the turtle above, is the "bite and spit" feeding method. The shark will charge an animal, take a bite, and then back off while the animal dies. This allows the shark to conserve energy because blood loss, rather than hard work, will eventually kill the prey.

only on sea urchins, and the whiskery shark, which feeds almost exclusively on octopus. The diet of sharks may also change as they mature. Young sandbar sharks primarily eat blue crabs, whereas the adults prey on offshore fishes and skates.

ON THE DEFENSE

Sharks are most at risk from predation by other sharks, but a few other fish, such as large gropers, are cause for concern. They employ various means of defense, from utilizing inbuilt physical features, to schooling, to avoidance, to the aggression that many larger, more active sharks display.

TAKING A POSITION

Aggression may sometimes mean outright attack, but it is more common that a shark will first signal its aggressive intentions in order to avoid attack. This signaling, or posturing, is known as agonistic behavior. Just as a wo will bare its teeth, arch its back, and lower its head to warn off an aggressor, a shark will use threatening postures t scare off an enemy. Th more agitated the shar becomes, the more intense the display. Sharks may also display aggression by "tai cracking," in whic the shark will swim directly a an animal posing a threat, and the suddenly turn away. As the shark turns, it flicks its tail, causing a loud crack which can startle potential predators.

Physical defense Some species have physical features which operate in times of threat.

UNDER THREAT In this side view of a gray reef shark (above), the top illustration shows the position the shark will adopt when threatened. It points its pectoral fins down, arches its back and moves its head from side to side. The illustration below shows the shark's posture in safety.

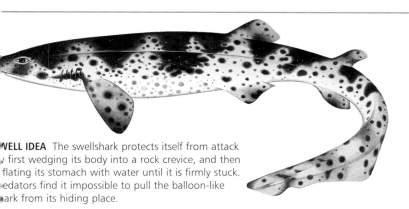

WELL IDEA The swellshark protects itself from attack by first wedging its body into a rock crevice, and then inflating its stomach with water until it is firmly stuck. Predators find it impossible to pull the balloon-like shark from its hiding place.

Dogfishes and hornsharks have hard, pointed spines in front of their dorsal fins. These spines make it difficult for a predator to consume the shark without injuring its mouth.

Camouflage is an effective means of defense for many species. The mottled coloration of wobbegong sharks and the weed-like tassels that surround their mouths make them very difficult to see as they rest in their reef habitat. Many other sharks also have striped, spotted, or blotchy skin patterns to provide camouflage, or coloration and shading that reduces their visibility in the water.

AVOIDANCE TECHNIQUES

Some sharks defend themselves by passive avoidance. Whitetip reef sharks, a small to medium-sized species that lives on coral reefs in the Indo-West Pacific, appear to defend themselves by remaining mostly inactive during daylight hours. They rest in caves and under ledges, where they are less likely to encounter predators. However, at night they become active, feeding aggressively on reef fishes and invertebrates. Generally, feeding at night is a popular defense strategy, and it has been noted that feeding activity increases on nights when there is no moonlight.

SOCIALIZING

Whereas many sharks appear to spend much of their time alone, some species are known to form large schools, often comprising single-sex and similar-sized individuals. The purpose of schooling among sharks is a point of speculation for researchers since, unlike smaller fishes, many species of shark do not need to form groups for protection from predators. Data about schooling behavior is hard to gather.

SOCIAL TYPES

Hammerhead sharks are known to school in the true sense of all members moving in the same direction, but some other species—including spiny dogfish, whiskery sharks, blacktip sharks, soupfin sharks, gummy sharks, bronze whalers, and juvenile dusky sharks—will often form aggregations. Large numbers of these species will congregate, mostly attracted by food, or the need to reproduce or migrate.

PUTTING THEIR HEADS TOGETHER Schooling is a social behavior of certain species, most notably hammerheads (shown to the right).

SECRET SOCIETY Whitetip sharks rest in small groups on the ocean floor, hidden under rocks and in caves. This behavior may be in order to protect each other from predators.

ierarchical order When groups
f sharks do gather to feed, a
istinct hierarchical order has
een observed, both within and
etween species, and even in
redominantly solitary species.
or example, it has been observed
at when feeding on schools of
sh, silvertip sharks dominate
alápagos sharks, and both
ominate blacktip sharks.

Pack hunting While most sharks
hunt alone, competing for food,
cooperative hunting does occur.
Sevengill sharks hunt in packs to
capture large fur seals, which, at up
to 775 pounds (350 kg), are more
than twice the weight of the largest
sevengill. By hunting as a group, a
pack of sevengill can attack and
consume an animal that a lone shark
could never overpower.

HANGERS ON

While most sharks are loners, they never really swim alone. Sharks carry a variety of marine passengers, inside and outside their bodies. Their parasites include many kinds of intestinal worm, as well as the leeches and crab-like copepods which live on a shark's skin—leeches near the mouth, and copepods near the gill slits, fins, and even on the eyes. Other creatures travel with a shark but do not feed from it.

These include pilot fishes, cleaner wrasse, and remoras. Pilot fish ride the pressure waves in front of a shark as it swims, and live on the leftovers of a shark's meal. Remoras and wrasse have a symbiotic relationship with a shark—they feed on the shark's parasites and the shark gets the benefit of a cleaning service.

ALL-DAY SUCKER Remoras, such as the one on the whale shark (below), use suction to attach, creating a vacuum with ridges of specialized muscle on their head.

OOSY TYPES Each of the eight species [of] remora attaches to a particular kind of [ho]st, some to sharks and rays, others to [sea] turtles, or jewfish (pictured below).

FOOD CHAIN Stripy cleaner wrasse, pictured above with a whitetip reef shark and below with a jewfish, feed off the parasites that live on these fishes.

REPRODUCTION

Most marine animals fertilize externally, releasing sperm and eggs into the water. A male shark, however, transfers sperm into a female's cloaca. The sperm then moves to the oviducal gland. As an ovulated egg passes through the oviducal gland, it is fertilized by stored sperm, and covered with an egg capsule. The eggs will develop in one of three main ways: placentally, feeding through an umbilical cord; within egg capsules that are laid in protecte[d] areas or anchored to a surface; or, most commonly, within very thin egg capsules that are retaine[d] inside the mother.

Courtship rituals In some speci[es] a male and female shark may perform a mating "dance" for ov[er] an hour, until the male signals h[is] intentions by biting the female. Mating scars—semicircular jaw impressions, slashes, and tooth nicks—can be seen on the back and pectoral fins of some female[s]

Female reproductive organs

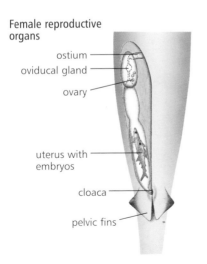

- ostium
- oviducal gland
- ovary
- uterus with embryos
- cloaca
- pelvic fins

Male reproductive organs

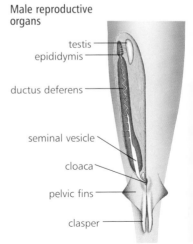

- testis
- epididymis
- ductus deferens
- seminal vesicle
- cloaca
- pelvic fins
- clasper

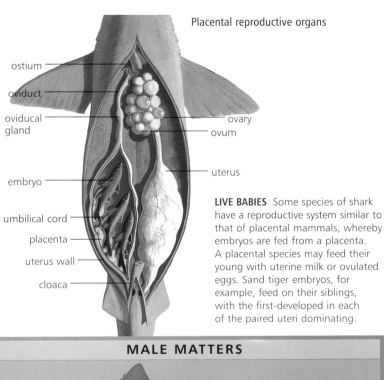

Placental reproductive organs

ostium

oviduct

oviducal gland

ovary

ovum

uterus

embryo

umbilical cord

placenta

uterus wall

cloaca

LIVE BABIES Some species of shark have a reproductive system similar to that of placental mammals, whereby embryos are fed from a placenta. A placental species may feed their young with uterine milk or ovulated eggs. Sand tiger embryos, for example, feed on their siblings, with the first-developed in each of the paired uteri dominating.

MALE MATTERS

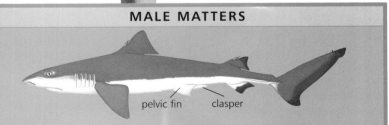

pelvic fin   clasper

Claspers, the male reproductive organs, are modified inner edges of pelvic fins. In mating, a single clasper is flared, rotated, and inserted into the female's cloaca.

GROWING UP

The gestation period of a shark embryo varies considerably between species, with the common range being from nine to twelve months. The shortest known gestation period is around five months for the bonnethead shark, and the longest is that of the spiny dogfish—at about 22 months. It is the longest known gestation period of any animal.

GROWTH RATES

Sharks grow fastest when they are young, reducing the amount of time they are vulnerable to predation. Species that are smallest at birth, such as the smooth dogfish, tend to grow fastest, some doubling in length by the time they are six months old, which is when they leave the inshore "nursery" grounds. Others, such as the large dusky shark, grow more steadily.

Reaching maturity

As sharks mature, their reproductive organs enlarge and become functional. A female's ovaries begin to develop yolky eggs that will go on to provide some, if not all, of the nutrition for the embryos. The claspers of the male shark grow in length, and the supporting cartilages become hardened by calcificatio to enable mating to occur. A grea deal of energy is then required for reproduction, so growth rates slow considerably. While most sharks reach maturity at five to ten years of age, small warm-water sharks often mature more rapidly, some within a year of birth, and large species may not fully develop until they are 20 years old or more.

neural canal

vertebral column

COUNTING THE YEARS
Like trees, the vertebra of sharks have concent bands that are laid down on a regular bas usually annually. By staining a cross-sectior the bands can be revealed and counted t estimate the shark's ag

RLY INDEPENDENCE Since sharks
•nd no time at all with their parents,
•ardless of whether they are born live,
• this lemon shark pup (above), or
•ched from an egg, their bodies are
•y formed and behavior at birth is
•ate. To help them survive until they
• adept at catching prey, a large
•ount of energy is stored in their liver.

ISTED START Hornsharks develop
•de a unique, oval egg case ringed
•h a spiral of ridges like a screw,
•ich the mother wedges into cracks
•d crevices. That is all the protection
•y, or any shark, will ever receive
•m their parents.

TRAVELING

Most sharks migrate annually. The distance they travel depends essentially on their swimming ability. While some species, such as the epaulette, may not migrate at all, powerful active species, such as the mako and blue sharks, may cross entire oceans.

WHY MIGRATE?

Sharks will often migrate to feed on specific fish. For example, great whites follow humpback whales to their summer calving grounds in order to feed on baby whales that are sick or stray too far from their mothers. Many sharks also demonstrate a preference for water of consisten temperature throughout the year and will travel in response to seasonal fluctuations in water temperature. Some species, such as soupfin sharks, migrate to a particular area to mate. The pregnant females will then trave again to a nursery location to pu

TAGGING

Tagged sharks have provided mo data about shark migrations. Recent tagging technologies include archival tags, which stor the animal's location each day, and satellite tags, which transmi their location to a satellite when ever the sharks break the surface

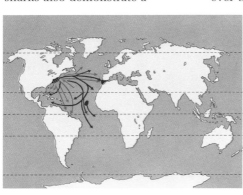

■ **BLUE TRAVELER** The blue sha (pictured top right) moves arou the Atlantic Ocean, venturing a far as Brazil, west Africa, and th Mediterranean Sea.

■ **MAKO MOVEMENTS** The ma shark (right) migrates individua from the northeast coast of the United States where it spends summer, to wintering grounds i warmer waters from the Gulf Stream to the Sargasso Sea.

SHARK MEETS HUMAN

On the attack. Uses and abuses.
Conserving and observing.

On the Attack

SHARK ATTACKS on humans are not common, and yet
we have an enduring fear of these animals. Perhaps this is
because on land humans have established their dominance
over every living creature, but in water we are literally out
of our depth. Even our superior intellect cannot deter sharks
from doing what they have always done in an environment
where we are very much the intruders.

FACT AND FICTION

Sharks are difficult and expensive to study, so there are large gaps in our knowledge about them. The image humans have of sharks is formed mostly by media reports on attacks, and a cycle is perpetuated—research on sharks is poorly funded because of their enduring negative reputation. So what is fact and what is fiction?

TELLING TRUTHS

Of the nearly 500 species of shark, more than 80 percent are smaller than humans, and are harmless to humans. The "average" shark is 3 to 4¼ feet (90 to 130 cm) long at maturity, i feeds on small fishes, crustacean and other small invertebrates, an it is more likely to avoid than attack a human.

Attack data In 1958, at the instigation of the United States Navy, a panel of scientists began to compile a worldwide historic database of shark attacks. By 1996, this database was known a the International Shark Attack File, and it contained more than 1,800 confirmed shark attacks. Between 75 and 100 new cases are added to the file each year, of which fewer than 20 are fatal.

HOLLYWOOD HYPE The 1974 movie *Jaws* used a great white shark (such as the on shown left) as a basis for the "man-eating" main character. The model built for the movie was 3 feet (90 cm) longer than the largest ever recorded real great white, and its teeth were deliberately over sized to enhance its fearsome appearance

Unfortunately, due to the difficulties of documenting attacks in developing countries, and the over-identification of one species—the great white—complete information on attacks worldwide still remains patchy.

Sharks in danger What we do now is that sharks probably attack fewer than a hundred people a year, yet people kill over a hundred million sharks in the same period. Uncontrolled, commercial fishing of sharks, the entanglement of sharks in

FALSE WITNESS There is some evidence to suggest that witnesses to attacks will identify the involvement of a great white shark because this is the type of shark they know best.

nets targeting other kinds of fishes, and escalating human encroachment into fragile coastal and riverine environments mean that we are killing sharks faster than they can reproduce. While fatal shark attacks are tragic, the bottom line is that sharks have much to more to fear from us than we do from them.

WHY ATTACK?

The majority of shark attacks occur where people and sharks are most likely to be in contact. It is believed that attacks involve one of two behaviors—defense or predation. On this basis, shark attacks are traditionally broken down into two main categories—provoked and unprovoked.

UNPROVOKED ATTACKS
Unprovoked attacks occur when victims blunder unintentionally into the behavioral sphere of a shark, and the shark perceives it is being threatened with harm. For example, a surfer or wind-surfer may speed into the area where a reef shark is swimming. The shark may lash out to defend itself.

Dining decisions Attacks on humans are also attributed to feeding behavior. It has been proposed that sharks mistake people splashing on the surface of the water for their usual prey. It is open to debate whether or not a shark actually mistakes a person for a particular kind of prey. It

may be enough that the person is at the surface of the water where many species find much of their food, whether it be fishes, marine mammals, or carrion. Attacks related to feeding, in which the shark approaches the victim as a potential meal, most often involve the larger species of sharks.

CONFUSING MESSAGES Viewed from below the ocean surface, a human paddling a board (above) resembles a large marine animal, such as a sea turtle (right). A shark that feeds on large items of prey might examine any such object.

PROVOKED ATTACKS

Provoked attacks are cases in which sharks defend themselves against deliberate or inadvertent human interference. While unfortunate, such attacks are not particularly surprising.

Shocking encounter Because underwater visibility is poor, divers are generally unaware of sharks until they are fairly close. In the majority of cases the shark will be more startled than the diver, and will flee. However, it appears that certain sharks act aggressively when approached too closely, and attacks may occur when a diver or swimmer is perceived as a threat. Gray reef sharks, in particular, exhibit a distinctive, agonistic display when they feel threatened, sometimes followed by a swift attack.

WHALE OF A RIDE The whale shark, the largest shark species in the world, does not have an aggressive nature, but it can lash out at a disturbance in its environment, causing accidental injury.

Error in judgment Experienced researchers, divers, and scientists approach all sharks with caution and respect. Provoked attacks that are related to threat or aggression are usually the result of humans showing poor judgment in relating to the sharks they encounter. Pulling the tail of a whitetip reef shark as it rests in an underwater cave, for example, or attempting to hand-feed it or members of other dangerous species, are examples of provocative behavior. If handled, even the bottom-dwelling, sluggish angelshark could deliver a terrible, if not fatal, bite with its small teeth.

DANGEROUS TYPES

Sharks tend to attack as individuals rather than in groups, and it is not always possible to determine exactly which species was responsible for a given attack. However, while more than 30 species of shark have been implicated in attacks on humans, the vast majority of fatal attacks appear to be carried out by only three of these—the white shark, tiger shark, and bull shark. None of these species includes humans as an important part of their diet. What makes these sharks dangerous to humans is their size, their varied diet, their

WHITE WORRY
The great white shark is believed to be the species most likely to attack people in temperate waters.

TROPICAL TERROR The tiger shark is probably responsible for the majority of attacks in tropical waters.

FRESHWATER FEAR Bull sharks, a coastal species, are also found in freshwater rivers and estuaries.

ability to capture large prey, their speed, and their tendency to inhabit near-shore areas.

Coast to open sea

White sharks are common on rocky shorelines, particularly where seals and sea lions crawl up onto shore—areas also favored by surfers and divers. Tiger sharks are often found around shallow reefs, harbors, and stream-mouths. Bull sharks are one of the few species that inhabit fresh-water habitats. The majority of open-ocean attacks are thought to be the work of oceanic whitetips, although blue sharks also pose a risk to people stranded at sea, for example, in boating or airplane accidents.

SPECIFIC SUSPECTS
Of the nine species of hammerhead sharks, only the great hammerhead is considered dangerous to humans.

WHAT HAPPENS IN AN ATTACK

Attacks can be categorized into a few main types. In a "hit-and-run" attack, usually a case of mistaken identity, the victim is quickly released and trauma is usually not too severe.

The most severe and fatal injuries result from aggressive "sneak" and "bump-and-bite" attacks, in which the shark circles, then bumps the victim before biting repeatedly.

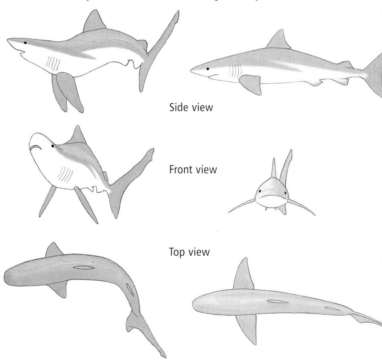

Side view

Front view

Top view

AGGRAVATED DISPLAY A threatened gray reef shark will display its aggression before attacking by arching its body and raising its head.

BITING ACTION

With the great white shark, the feeding action begins when the head and snout are lifted, and the lower jaw is simultaneously depressed. Once the jaw is fully open, muscle contractions force the forward rotation of the upper jaw, which detaches from the skull and comes completely out of the mouth. This action creates the predator's awesome bite.

A similarity between encounters with both humans and marine animals is that the initial attack frequently involves a single, massive bite that inflicts a major, often fatal, injury. Usually no flesh is removed until the subsequent bites. This predatory behavior, unique to great whites, has led researchers to propose the "bite and spit" hypothesis. The prey is released after the first quick and powerful bite, aimed to incapacitate the victim. This behavior is thought to conserve energy, and reduce the chance of injury to the shark during, for example, prolonged contact with a large, struggling elephant seal.

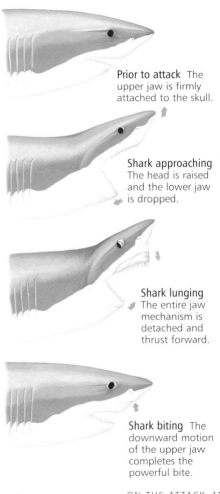

Prior to attack The upper jaw is firmly attached to the skull.

Shark approaching The head is raised and the lower jaw is dropped.

Shark lunging The entire jaw mechanism is detached and thrust forward.

Shark biting The downward motion of the upper jaw completes the powerful bite.

CHANCES OF ATTACK

Per capita, the greatest recorded number of shark attacks have occurred in Australia, the United States, and South Africa. These countries all have extensive coastlines within the peak latitudes of 32°N and 34°S—the area most densely populated by both humans and sharks—and have seasonally warm water temperatures. Worldwide figures almost certainly underestimate the number of attacks in developing and non-English speaking countries, which are less likely to make formal reports.

SHORE BREAKERS

A breakdown of recent figures for shark attacks worldwide shows that swimmers are the most frequently attacked group, followed by surfboard riders, spearfishers, snorkelers, scuba divers, anglers, and boaters.

Close calls Most shark attacks occur close to shore, with approximately 31 percent of victims being within 50 feet (15 m) of the water's edge and 62 percent being in water that is less than 5 feet (1.5 m) deep. These figures are not surprising, given that most people who enter

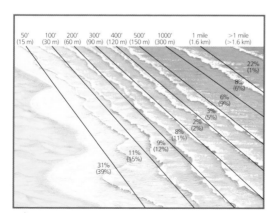

| 50'
(15 m) | 100'
(30 m) | 200'
(60 m) | 300'
(90 m) | 400'
(120 m) | 500'
(150 m) | 1000'
(300 m) | 1 mile
(1.6 km) | >1 mile
(>1.6 km) |

22%
(1%)

8%
(6%)

6%
(9%)

3%
(5%)

2%
(2%)

8%
(11%)

9%
(12%)

11%
(15%)

31%
(39%)

DISTANCE BREAKDOWN This graph shows shark attacks relative to distance from shore, and (in brackets) the percentage of people who swim at these distances.

RELATIVE DANGER A human is 16.5 times more likely to be hit by lightning than to be attacked by a shark, and 5 times more likely to die from a lightning injury than from a shark bite.

the water for recreational activities seldom venture far offshore, and sharks frequently inhabit coastal areas. More than 90 percent of reported attacks occur on the surface. This reflects the habits of recreational water-users, but also suggests the importance of feeding behavior in understanding attacks.

Coast to open sea People stranded in the open ocean following boat or air disasters are particularly vulnerable to attack because they are often injured and bleeding, and floating on the surface with no protection. This is confirmed by events such as the sinking of the USS *Indianapolis*, at the end of World War II, which left some 800 men stranded in the tropical Pacific Ocean for nearly a week. More than half the men died, and sharks are believed responsible for about 100 of these deaths.

AVOIDING ATTACK

Whether swimming, surfing, diving, or even observing sharks from the safety of a cage, there are some commonsense precautionary rules that can be observed to avoid attack.

BASIC RULES

The most basic key to avoiding shark attack is to understand and respect the shark's environment. When visiting a new area, seek local advice and always heed current shark warnings. If diving, find out what kinds of sharks you are likely to encounter and learn about each species' behavior.

Bodily fluids Avoid entering the water with an open wound; sharks may be attracted to blood and other kinds of bodily fluids.

For this reason, too, avoid areas where people are fishing. When spearfishing, store any catch

CAGED SAFETY A shark cage is the best way to avoid attack when observing large sharks in their own environment.

DIVER BEWARE Basic precautionary rules should be observed even from inside a cage. The diver should keep still, and let the shark investigate on its own terms.

...arefully to avoid filling the water with blood.

afe times Avoid entering the water at dawn, dusk, and at night, when sharks are most active and visibility is limited. Similarly, avoid swimming or diving in murky waters, particularly after storms and in near-flooding rivers.

tay together Avoid being in the water alone, though divers should not cluster. Sharks seem to perceive tightly packed groups of divers as a single, large, noisy, unfamiliar, and therefore frightening, organism.

ace to face If you do meet a shark, do not shout at it, and do not attempt to push at it, punch it, or hit it. Keep your movements slow and deliberate; quick movement may cause the shark to become fearful and provoke a defensive attack. If possible, reduce your vertical profile because sharks seem more unnerved by height than length. Divers can do this by crouching on the ocean floor. It is important not to lose sight of the shark, but avoid direct eye contact.

Personal Protection

■ Skin and scuba divers run a risk of being attacked because their activities increase the possibility of encounters with sharks. Several weapons have been developed for divers to use against sharks, many of them originating with the United States Navy in an effort to protect their personnel from shark attack.

CHEMICAL REPELLENT Shark Chaser, a package of copper acetate and nigrosine dye, was issued to Allied personnel during World War II, but it proved ineffective.

ANTI-SHARK WEAPONS

Of use to recreational divers is the shark billy—a pole with a sharp point to keep sharks at bay—and the bang stick—a pole with an explosive device that will kill a shark when banged against it. The drawbacks of these weapons are that they may injure the diver, and they are only of use if the shark is seen on approach.

Electrical field The most effective recent deterrent is the Protective Oceanic Device (POD), which was developed by the Natal Sharks Board of South Africa. This battery-powered device attaches to a scuba tank and produces a strong electric field around a person. When a

EFFECTIVE DEVICE The shark POD was designed to repel the three most dangerous sharks—the bull, great white, and tiger sharks—and represents the most effective shark deterrent yet developed for divers.

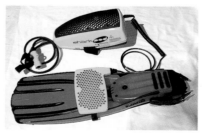

INFLATABLE SAFETY The Johnson Shark Bag fits into a small pack and can be inflated in an emergency. The bag fully encloses the diver. Underwater, it protects protruding limbs that may invite an exploratory bite.

ark encounters the field, it is
pelled. The device is effective
a distance of about 23 feet
m), but has not yet been
oven to deter large sharks
feeding mode.

emical efforts A problem with
chemical repellents developed
d tested to date is that far too
eat quantities are needed to
oduce the desired effect. One
ea of research, however,
volves a group of chemicals
lled surfactants (which cause
e foaming action in many soaps
d detergents), discovered in
small fish that sharks are
luctant to bite. The strategy
ing tested with a surfactant is
inject it into the shark's mouth,
us producing the very high
ncentration required.

REINFORCED PROTECTION A diver suit made of a modern form of chain mail provides effective protection against sharks the size of this 6-foot (2-m) blue.

Public Protection

■ Most shark attacks occur at bathing beaches, simply because of the number of people there. The most effective way to protect beaches is to fence or wall in a bathing area in order to physically prevent sharks from entering. However, these closures protect only small portions of the shoreline.

SHUTTING THEM OUT

Physically excluding sharks most often involves stretching long nets across the mouths of bays with swimming beaches. This method has been used particularly effectively in Australia, South Africa, and New Zealand, but is not more widely utilized because of economic considerations. Initial construction costs are high because netting is labor intensive. In addition, the nets n to be checked regularly—daily if possible—and require ongoing maintenance and repair work, ar often reinstallation after damage caused by heavy storms.

New ideas Traditional eradicatic programs use large-sized mesh n to both protect swimmers and tra sharks, with the unfortunate by-product that other kinds of marir life, such as fishes, turtles, birds even whales, become entangled die. Trials are currently underwa using acoustic signals to warn ba whales away from shark nets.

DOUBLE ACTION In Natal, Africa, the nets are set in two staggered rows beyond the surfline and are serviced regularly by meshing teams working from skiiboats.

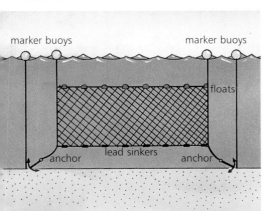

marker buoys · marker buoys

floats

lead sinkers

anchor · anchor

SETTING UP Netting set-ups vary according to the area. Some nets (pictured above) are set almost to the ground, while others (pictured left) sit above the sea bed. Generally, however, each end of a net is secured by an anchor and its position is marked by floats, which also help to hold the net upright.

WORLD ATTACK

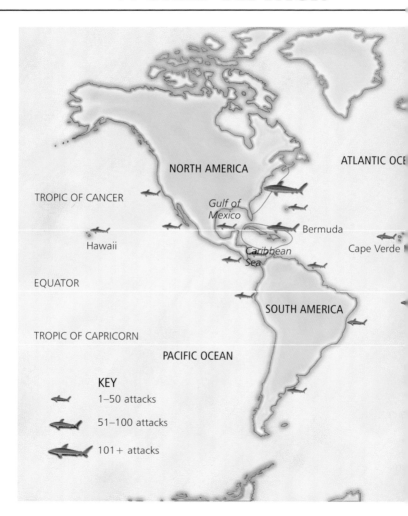

NORTH AMERICA

ATLANTIC OCE

TROPIC OF CANCER

Gulf of Mexico

Bermuda

Hawaii

Cape Verde

Caribbean Sea

EQUATOR

SOUTH AMERICA

TROPIC OF CAPRICORN

PACIFIC OCEAN

KEY

1–50 attacks

51–100 attacks

101+ attacks

EUROPE

ASIA

Japan

rranean
ea

Persian
Gulf

India

Red Sea

CA

Philippines

Papua New
Guinea

INDIAN OCEAN

Pacific
Islands

ulu
l

AUSTRALIA

New
Zealand

ACK DISTRIBUTION This map shows
relative worldwide distribution of
henticated cases of shark attacks
humans that are recorded in the
ernational Shark Attack File.

SOUTHERN
OCEAN

North America

■ The rate of shark attacks on humans in United States waters is climbing, reflecting an increase in human population, and a surge in the popularity of water sports.

Leading state Florida leads the region in shark attacks, with an average of 17 attacks per year since 1990. The high number of attacks in Florida is attributable in part to its very long coastline and inshore waters that are high in biological productivity and habitat diversity. The shark fauna is rich and populations, until recently, have been robust.

Pacific coast California leads al eastern Pacific areas, averaging three confirmed reports of encounters with sharks per year since 1990. Shark attacks are rar in the cold waters of the Pacific Northwest, and California's cool waters attract few large, inshore shark species—most attacks are credited to the great white shark Attacks occur year round, but most have been recorded from the warmer months of July to October, coinciding with observe times of peak white shark and human abundance.

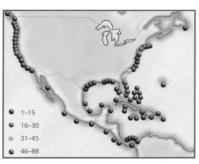

UNPROVOKED ATTACKS To 1999, there were 703 unprovoked attacks in the North American region. This includes attacks related to spearfishing and diving.

Legend:
- 1–15
- 16–30
- 31–45
- 46–88

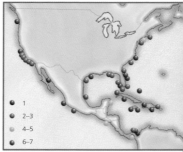

FATAL UNPROVOKED ATTACKS To 1999, there were 87 deaths in the region attributable to unprovoked shark attac This is 12 percent of the total attacks.

Legend:
- 1
- 2–3
- 4–5
- 6–7

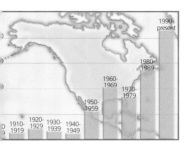

ATTACKS OVER TIME The graph (left) shows the number of recorded unprovoked attacks in North and Central American waters in 10-year spans from 1890 to the present. The higher number of recent attacks reflects the greater number of people using the oceans for recreation since the late 1800s (represented below).

■ While shark stocks in the region are declining, the human population is on an upward spiral, with synchronous increases in marine recreational activities. Such aquatic sports as surfboard riding, sailboarding, kayaking, and skin and scuba diving have become increasingly popular in all waters of North America, resulting in increased opportunities for humans to come into contact with sharks. This situation is reflected in statistics showing a higher number of recent shark attacks.

Beach attacks Attacks are known from a wide variety of habitats, but they occur most frequently off beaches, from just beyond the surfline to the wash zone. This area is highly utilized by waders, swimmers, and surfers. Attacks that occur on reefs and in the open ocean are primarily on divers and are fewer in number.

AQUATIC ACTIVITY

When the region is looked at as a whole, attack victims are engaged about equally in three recreational activities: surfing (including rafting and kayaking), swimming (including floating and wading), and diving (scuba and snorkeling). However, there are marked differences in activity emphasis within the region, with

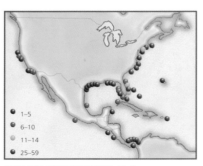

ATTACKS ON SWIMMERS Swimmers on the Atlantic coast are twice as vulnerable to shark attack as those in Pacific waters.

ATTACKS ON DIVERS The Pacific coast is three times more likely to be dangerous for divers than Atlantic waters.

e Atlantic more dangerous for
rfers and swimmers, and the
acific more dangerous for divers.
he Pacific coast is colder, and
ome to great whites. Humans
ecome vulnerable when they
lapt to these conditions by
earing wetsuits.

ender bias The data on attacks
ggests that sharks are gender
discriminate, attacking people
the proportion they appear in
e water. Aquatic recreation,
pecially surfing and diving, has
storically been dominated by
ales and Caucasians. Regionally,
) percent of the attacks on
mans have been on males and
) percent on Caucasians.

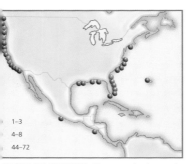

1–3
4–8
44–72

TACKS ON SURFERS Unprovoked attacks
surfers occur with much greater
ensity on the Atlantic coastline.

RECREATIONAL ACTIVITY Victims of shark
attack are likely to be involved in
swimming, surfing, or diving.

■ Correct identification of many species of shark is difficult even for trained scientists carefully examining a specimen, so it is challenging to identify the attacking species of shark from the often sketchy description given. Nevertheless, based on more than 200 positive identifications, a large suite of species has been implicated in attacks in the region.

BULL SHARK ATTACKS Bull sharks are the second most frequently identified attackers in Atlantic waters.

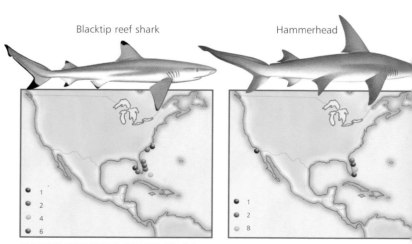

Blacktip reef shark

Hammerhead

BLACKTIP REEF SHARK ATTACKS Blacktip reef sharks are the most frequently identified attackers in Atlantic waters.

HAMMERHEAD SHARK ATTACKS Hammerheads have been implicated in unprovoked attacks.

CARIBBEAN REEF SHARK ATTACKS Attacks by Caribbean reef sharks are most likely to occur in southern insular areas.

SPINNER SHARK ATTACKS Spinner sharks are the third most frequently identified attackers in Atlantic waters.

Tiger shark

Great white

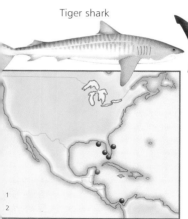

TIGER SHARK ATTACKS Tiger sharks regularly enter shallow waters and are considered extremely dangerous.

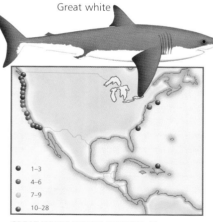

- 1–3
- 4–6
- 7–9
- 10–28

GREAT WHITE SHARK ATTACKS The number of divers meeting great whites underwater is increasing.

Australia

■ Australia currently has one of the highest rates of shark attack, and claims many of the most recent attacks. Before the introduction of meshing, it had the highest rate worldwide.

FINDINGS AND THEORIES

One of the most comprehensive studies of shark attack in Australia is that done by Dr. Victor Coppleson, which he completed in 1958. Most of Coppleson's findings still apply,

including the discoveries that attacks most often occur between two and six o'clock in the afternoon, and that weather, tide and water clarity were not factor that influenced attacks. One of h most significant findings was the the majority of Australian attack were made by lone sharks, and

ONE-OFF ATTACK The blue shark (below an efficient open-ocean predator, has been identified in only one attack in Australian waters.

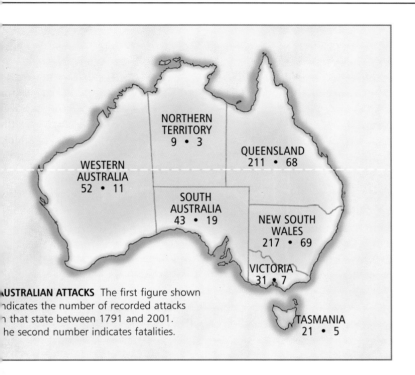

AUSTRALIAN ATTACKS The first figure shown indicates the number of recorded attacks in that state between 1791 and 2001. The second number indicates fatalities.

NORTHERN TERRITORY
9 • 3

WESTERN AUSTRALIA
52 • 11

QUEENSLAND
211 • 68

SOUTH AUSTRALIA
43 • 19

NEW SOUTH WALES
217 • 69

VICTORIA
31 • 7

TASMANIA
21 • 5

that only in a few instances were shark packs involved. He found that in many cases, the shark would strike the same victim twice, or more often, while completely ignoring other swimmers nearby. Dr. Coppleson developed the "rogue shark" theory, which holds that individual sharks may develop a taste for attack, and that a single shark may be responsible for several attacks in an area. The theory has yet to be proven, but has been raised again in relation to a recent spate of attacks.

■ At May 7, 2001, the Australian Shark Attack File had recorded 584 shark attacks in Australian waters (including Torres Strait Islands, Cocos Islands, and within the 200 nautical mile international fishing zone), of which 182 had been fatal. The total number of recorded attacks includes unprovoked and provoked encounters, bites while removing sharks from nets, bites on kayaks and small canoes, and bites from sharks in captivity.

Dangerous activities According to the File, swimming was by far the most dangerous activity. The second most dangerous activity was surfboard riding. Scuba diving, spearfishing, and snorkeling figured prominently on the list of activities in which sharks were encountered.

In comparison Fatalities resulting from shark attack are extremely rare compared with other kinds of fatalities in water-related activities. Between 1968 and 1991 in New South Wales, 121 rock fishermen were swept off the rocks and drowned and 37 surfboard riders drowned. In that same period, 32 shark encounters were recorded with only one fatality reported. On average, less than one person per year has been killed by shark attack in Australia over the last 200 years.

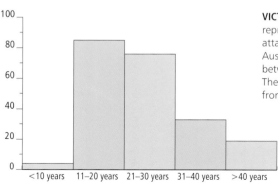

VICTIM'S AGE This graph represents 217 cases of attack recorded in the Australian Shark Attack File between 1791 and 1998. The age of the victims range from 7 to 70 years.

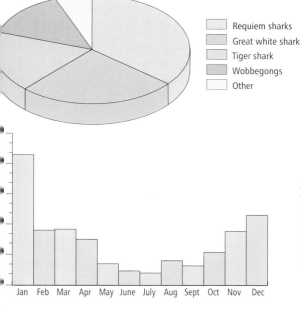

SPECIES CHART
This pie chart represents the most common shark species in 168 attacks between 1791 and 1998.

- Requiem sharks
- Great white shark
- Tiger shark
- Wobbegongs
- Other

COMMON MONTH
The most common month of attack in 527 cases reported between 1791 and 1998 is represented in this graph (left).

Jan Feb Mar Apr May June July Aug Sept Oct Nov Dec

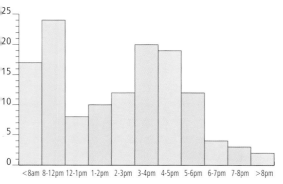

25
20
15
10
5
0

<8am 8-12pm 12-1pm 1-2pm 2-3pm 3-4pm 4-5pm 5-6pm 6-7pm 7-8pm >8pm

COMMON TIME
The most common time of attack in 131 cases reported between 1791 and 1998 is represented in this graph (left).

A common perception is that sharks attack people only to eat them. Of the sharks that have been identified in attacks in Australian waters (pictured here), only the behavior of the great white, which is implicated in more attacks than any other shark, is probably directly related to feeding. This is because these sharks habitually prey on large marine animals.

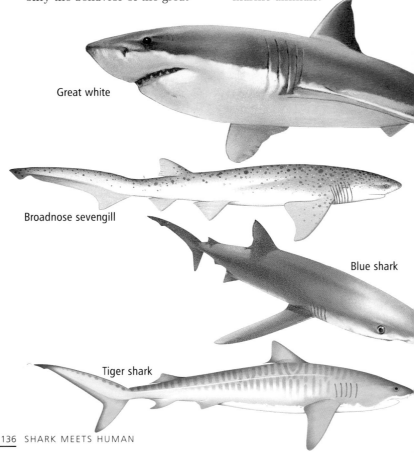

Great white

Broadnose sevengill

Blue shark

Tiger shark

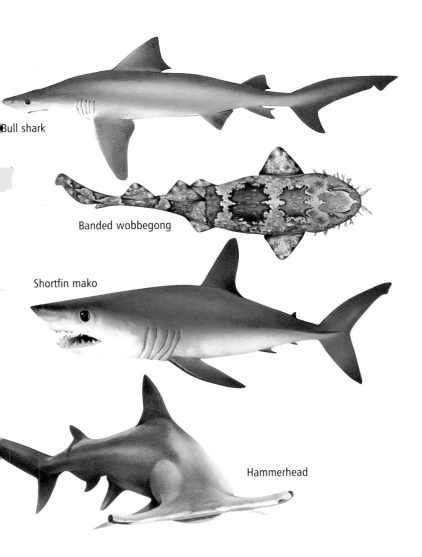

Bull shark

Banded wobbegong

Shortfin mako

Hammerhead

South Africa

■ Like Australia, South Africa has an unenviable record for shark attacks. All eight of the major orders of sharks, and almost all the families, occur along the South African coastline—some 111 species of shark. However, vigorous anti-shark measures, such as netting, in recent times have significantl reduced the risks to water-users. The pattern of attack may be correlated with temperature. No attacks on water-users have beer

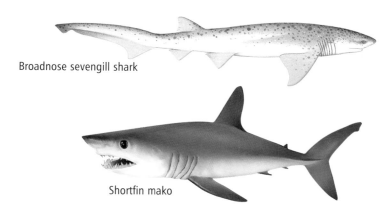

Tiger shark

Broadnose sevengill shark

Shortfin mako

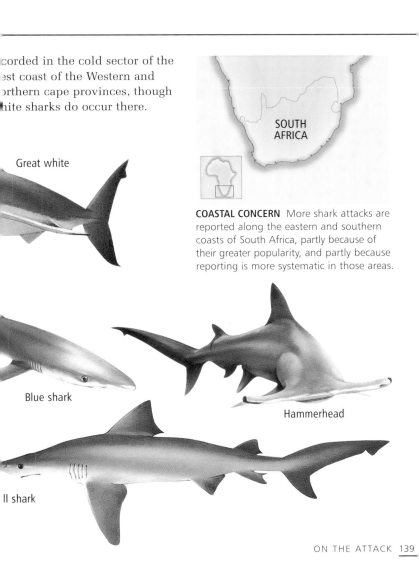

corded in the cold sector of the
est coast of the Western and
orthern cape provinces, though
hite sharks do occur there.

Great white

SOUTH
AFRICA

COASTAL CONCERN More shark attacks are
reported along the eastern and southern
coasts of South Africa, partly because of
their greater popularity, and partly because
reporting is more systematic in those areas.

Blue shark

Hammerhead

ll shark

New Zealand

■ Despite the number of potentially dangerous species found around the coastline of New Zealand, and the popularity of recreational water use, shark attacks are rare. There have been only 10 fatal shark attacks recorded in 130 years. There is some evidence of a rise in seawater temperatures and this has been linked to increased numbers and wider distribution.

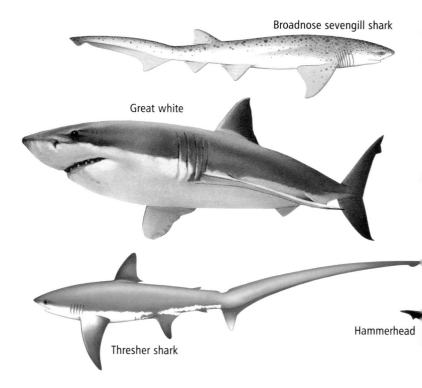

Broadnose sevengill shark

Great white

Thresher shark

Hammerhead

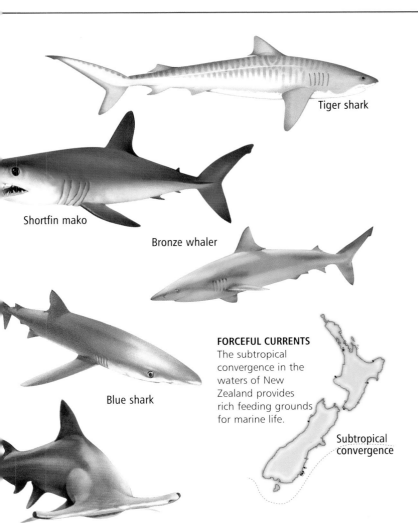

Tiger shark

Shortfin mako

Bronze whaler

Blue shark

FORCEFUL CURRENTS
The subtropical convergence in the waters of New Zealand provides rich feeding grounds for marine life.

Subtropical convergence

Uses and Abuses

THE DEMAND FOR SHARK products is booming. Almost a million tons of shark are harvested annually by fisheries worldwide, both as targeted catch and as unintended by-catch. Now demand is outstripping supply, and overfishing threatens both the industry and the sharks themselves.

SHARK PRODUCTS

Sharks have historically provided a remarkable array of products useful to humans, and modern medical science is still discovering a host of benefits. It is a peculiar characteristic of the corneas of shark eyes that they do not swell when placed in varying concentrations of salt solutions. Consequently, sharks' corneas have been used as successful substitutes for human corneas. Powdered shark cartilage is used in non-traditional medicines as an anti-inflammatory agent for the treatment of arthritis, wound

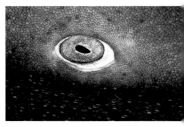

MEDICAL MARVELS Modern science is experimenting with, and using, corneas of sharks in human corneal transplants

healing after surgery, and to enhance the body's immune response against tumors. Shark liver oil, once prized as a

USEFUL PARTS The body parts of sharks are utilized in a variety of industries, from medicine to tourism.

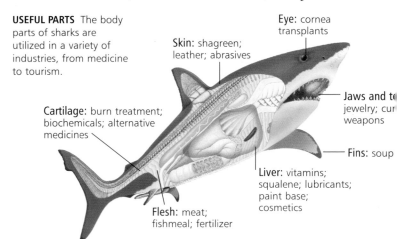

Eye: cornea transplants

Skin: shagreen; leather; abrasives

Jaws and te jewelry; cur weapons

Cartilage: burn treatment; biochemicals; alternative medicines

Fins: soup

Liver: vitamins; squalene; lubricants; paint base; cosmetics

Flesh: meat; fishmeal; fertilizer

bricant and source of Vitamin has recently attracted interest r its pharmaceutical properties. ualene, a compound found in e liver oil of deep-sea sharks, now being used in cosmetics, armaceuticals, and as a bricant in machinery.

Another product of shark ver oil, diacyl glycerol ether AGE), is used in the treatment wounds and burns, and a bstance derived from shark rtilage is used as artificial skin r burn victims.

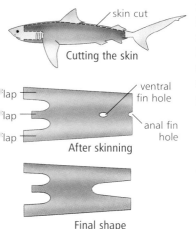

skin cut

Cutting the skin

lap
lap
lap

ventral fin hole

anal fin hole

After skinning

Final shape

SHARK ART AND CUISINE

The most characteristic feature of shark skin is its roughness, resulting from the placoid scales, or denticles, embedded in the skin. Dried skin—called shagreen—was once used for polishing wood, although it has been supplanted by glasspaper, or carborundum sheets. European artisans used treated shagreen for binding books, and to decorate sword hilts and sheaths. Today, it is used worldwide to make shoes, belts, handbags, and wallets. Shark teeth, traditionally used by Pacific Islanders to make and decorate tools and weapons, are still used today in tourist replicas of these items, and for jewelry.

Shark liver oil

SPECIALTY LEATHER Shark leather generally has a higher tensile strength than leather made from cattle hides. Boroso leather, made from the shagreen of small sharks by lightly polishing the scales to a high gloss, is an expensive specialty product.

In cuisines as different as Serbian and Vietnamese, Jamaican and Javanese, shark has appeared on the menu for centuries, with each culture's preparation giving the flesh specific local flavor. Western consumers, who in the past generally considered the flesh to be inferior—and marketed it under alternative names, such as "rock salmon" and "flake"—are now buying it with enthusiasm.

The fins of sharks—tough, gristly protruberances with little if any, nutritional value—play a unique role in Chinese cuisine. Historically, they have been eagerly sought by gourmets for specialist dishes, for which merchants, and consumers, will pay a fortune. Hong Kong is the biggest world market for shark fins, with some 60 countries exporting fins to it. Usually only

e first dorsal fin, the pectoral [fi]ns, and the lower lobe of the [ca]udal (tail) fin are used for [m]aking soup. The price paid [de]pends on size, color, species, [cu]t, trim, and moisture content. [In] soup, only the horny fibers [in] the fin are used, compressed [in]to fibrous mats which add a [gl]utinous texture to the dish.

[GA]M FISH The flesh of the sharks [pic]tured below is tasty and nutri-[tio]us, and is sold in fishmarkets [aro]und the world.

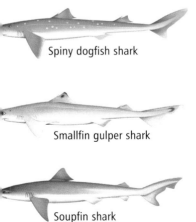

Spiny dogfish shark

Smallfin gulper shark

Soupfin shark

FINS TO MARKET The modern demand for shark fins (being harvested above, and seen drying far left) has made them a valuable commodity, exported from countries worldwide to the Asian markets.

FISHING METHODS

Sharks are captured using a variety of fishing methods, according to the species targeted and the habitat in which they live. Coastal sharks are most often captured with gillnets set on the seabed, or with longlines. Gillnets form an invisible barrier into which the shark swims, becoming either gilled (caught by the head and gills), or entangled by the fins and body. Longlines consist of a mainline with short lines attached along its length, each of which ends in a baited hook. To capture open-ocean sharks, longlines or gillnets are set in waters close to the surface.

Some small schooling sharks, such as spiny dogfish and angel-sharks, are captured by trawling giant mesh bags over the seabed to scoop them up. Deep-water trawl fisheries, targeting fishes

UNNECESSARY DEATH A Port Jackson shark and an angelshark are entangled in a discarded fishing net.

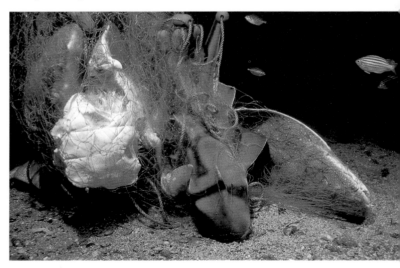

uch as orange roughy, often
nintentionally catch substantial
umbers of deep-water sharks.
he two largest shark species,
asking and whale sharks, are
ometimes captured by small-
cale traditional fisheries using
arpoons. Large, acrobatic sharks,
uch as mako sharks, are popular
vith sport fisheries, and anglers
ay large sums for a chance to
atch them.

Commercial failure In the face
f unrelenting demand, there are
ew convincing examples of a
ustainable shark fishery on a

CAREFUL CATCH Capturing a shark
without killing it, or damaging its body,
is an expensive, labor-intensive process.

modern, commercial scale.
Most shark fisheries that have
been established have initially
boomed and then collapsed as
a result of overfishing and poor
management. The basking shark
fishery of Achill Island, off the
coast of western Europe, is a
typical example. Between 1950
and 1955, over 1,000 sharks were
landed each year. By the early
1960s, the fishery had crashed.

A Threatened Resource

Shark populations are declining worldwide at alarming rates, due to over-fishing, by-catch fishing, and human encroachment into shark habitats. Sharks are among the ocean's top predators; their demise threatens the balance of life in the sea.

LONG-TERM VIEW
The increasing demand for shark products, particularly fins, has made it worthwhile retaining parts of the sharks taken as by-catch. Because the economic significance of shark fishing is relatively small, few agencies are willing to fund research into the management of fisheries. The result is overfishing, and an increase in disturbing practices such as finning, whereby a shark fins are cut off at sea. For many species of shark, the only hope of long-term survival is that consumer demand for shark product diminishes.

ENVIRONMENTAL THREA
Pollution from oil spills and industrial waste, as well as coastal construction, are threatening the viability some shark populations particularly in sheltered bays that are favored shark nursery areas.

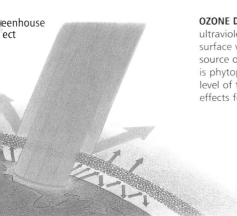

eenhouse
ect

OZONE DEPLETION Increases in the ultraviolet radiation that penetrates surface waters can affect the primary source of food for marine animals, which is phytoplankton. Any changes at this level of the food chain have flow-on effects for sharks.

PEST CONTROL Sharks are under pressure from eradication programs which try to remove the threat of specific "dangerous" species, such as the great white shark (below).

Conserving
and Observing

THE MORE WE KNOW, the better equipped we are to deal with sharks rationally and responsibly. Reliable information is reaching us through innovative research, through an entertainment market that competes to provide exciting images, and through the tourism industry, which increasingly is providing the means for humans to view sharks in the wild.

WORKING WITH SHARKS

Until the last few decades, most of what we learned about sharks was derived from the study of dead specimens. By dissecting dead sharks, scientists were able to determine basic information, such as their internal anatomy, the structure of their skeletons and sensory systems, their diet, their method of tooth replacement, and their various reproductive strategies.

Early research Some of the earliest studies of live sharks were funded by the United States Navy, which was concerned by the threats sharks posed to its personnel and equipment. This research focused on the sensory biology of sharks, with the ultimate goal being the development of an effective shark repellent. Much of this research was conducted in tanks or shallow pens near

IN THE WILD Observing sharks in the wild can be difficult and dangerous, but makes a significant contribution.

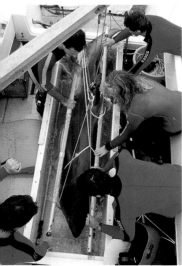

DIFFICULT MISSION Capturing a shark for experimentation may involve constraint in a sling (above), then sedation and placement in an on-board tank (left).

the shore, where the ability of sharks to see, smell, taste, and detect electric fields was tested. **New goal** The research of the 1960s and 1970s was driven by the desire to protect humans from sharks; now research is more inspired by the need to protect sharks from humans— to learn about their biology and patterns of migration so that the remaining populations can be protected.

EXPERIMENTS

Tagging sharks reveals how far they travel and how much of the ocean a particular species uses, by comparing where a shark is tagged and where it is recaptured. It can also indicate which countries' fisheries are exploiting a common resource. Information such as growth rates and longevity can also be determined—vital for gauging the resilience of a species to fishing pressure, and for calculating sustainable catch rates.

DATA TRANSMISSION
To obtain more detailed information than tag-and-release experiments can offer, transmitters are placed on, or in, some sharks. Depth-sensitive transmitters measure not only the horizontal movements of sharks, but also the depth and temperature at which they are located. Such data is important for understanding which part of the ocean habitat a shark uses, and may ultimately help reduce shark by-catch and protect shark nursery grounds.

Close calls Because radio waves do not penetrate salt water, transmitters for tracking sharks rely on ultrasound. Such transmitters have a range of only about 2,600 feet (800 m), which means that the tracking boat must stay close to the shark, not always an easy task in rough water.

THICK-SKINNED Because sharks are large and their skin is thick and quick to heal, is easy and painless for them to be fitted with transmitters and tags so that they can be tracked and monitored over tim

EXTENDED RESEARCH Sharks have been at the forefront of both tagging and tracking technology, and procedures used on them have since been applied to other open-ocean fishes, such as tuna.

PURPOSE BUILT The method used to attach a transmitter is adapted to suit the type of shark, and the conditions in which it is found. For example, juvenile hammerheads can be caught and force-fed a transmitter through a tube. Tiger sharks are surgically implanted after being turned upside down, which renders them virtually immobile. In other cases, the transmitters must be harpooned into place (left).

FILMING

Film, video, and still photography are all used extensively in the study of sharks. By analyzing high-speed video footage of sharks feeding, scientists have studied how sharks hunt and kill their prey. This approach was used to reveal the awesome biting action of the white shark.

PHOTO IDENTIFICATION

Still photography has been used to identify individual white sharks. This is an adaptation of a technique used first for whales,

LIGHTS... CAMERA... Underwater photographers (top and below right) often attach strobe lights to the camera to artificially light marine subjects, such as these whitetip reef sharks (below).

hich uses the fact that the
orsal and caudal fins of white
arks have distinctive features
at remain unchanged over time.
ese fins break the water when
e sharks feed, allowing them to
photographed from a boat. The
otographs enable the sharks to
reliably identified years later,
oviding useful information
out their distribution and
igration patterns. An advantage
this method over tagging is that
e sharks need not be captured,
d the problem of tags being
ed is avoided.

Innovative approaches While
filming sharks has useful research
applications, much of the work
done in this area is aimed at the
entertainment market. The
growing popularity of shark
documentaries has led to a
demand for dramatic footage.
Recent innovations include
mounting downward-looking
cameras inside surfboards to
record the upward feeding charge
of white sharks, and tethering
miniature video cameras onto the
backs of large sharks to provide a
unique perspective of their world.

SHARK VIEWING

In some areas, access to sharks may be fairly easily gained, and little planning is required. Caribbean reef sharks in the Bahamas, for example, can be found there all year round, and day trips provided by local dive centers, or dive resorts, will virtually guarantee sightings. However, many species are not only unique to the waters of certain countries, but they may gather in an area for only limited seasons. The whale sharks at Ningaloo Reef in Western Australia are an excellent example of this—they congregate there only during late March, April, and May. To experience the thrill of diving with them may involve traveling long distances. Some sharks are found only in remote locations. To see the silvertip sharks in Papua New Guinea, or the sharks in the Galápagos Islands, requires a boat trip on a live-aboard dive boat for 7 to 10 days to reach the area.

Careful planning—even for experienced divers—is essential to ensure that an encounter with

RARE BEAUTY Whitetip reef sharks can be found in the isolated caves of the Galápagos Islands. Due to strong currents, and little or no diving support through the hotels and guesthouses, this area is not suitable for novice divers.

arks is safe, environmentally und, exciting, and memorable. me dive operations feature ve guides that hand-feed sharks. ologists strongly advise against is interruption of the shark's tural behavior—and not just cause of the danger it presents divers. They are concerned out the changes that occur shark behavior and ecology hen they are "trained," through repetition, to approach divers, and to gather at the sound of boat engines. The best course of action is to relax and observe the sharks without interacting with them.

BOUNTIFUL REEF Good conditions almost all year round make the Great Barrier Reef, off the northeast coast of Australia, a popular site for viewing not only sharks, but all kinds of marine life.

Shark Viewing Sites

1. San Diego, USA	11. Similan and Surin Islands, Thailand
2. Kona Coast, Hawaii, USA	12. Yap and Palau, Micronesia
3. Sea of Cortez, Mexico	13. Rangiroa Atoll, French Polynesia
4. Revillagigedo Islands, Mexico	14. Mamanuca Islands, Fiji
5. Cocos Island, Costa Rica	15. Valerie's Reef, Papua New Guinea
6. The Bahamas	16. Ningaloo Reef, Australia
7. Galápagos Islands, Ecuador	17. Neptune Islands, Australia
8. Isle of Man, UK	18. Great Barrier Reef, Australia
9. Râs Muhammad, Egypt	19. New South Wales, Australia
10. Cape Town, South Africa	20. Lord Howe Island, Australia

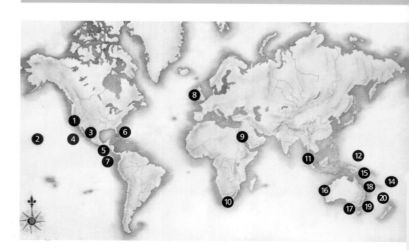

THE WILD The growing fascination with sharks is reflected in the increasing mber of people paying to dive with them in their natural environment. s scuba diver is swimming with a potentially dangerous blue shark.

SHARK
SHOWCASE

Classifying sharks.
Hexanchiformes. Squaliformes.
Pristiophoriformes, Squatiniformes,
Heterodontiformes. Orectolobiformes.
Lamniformes. Carcharhiniformes.

USING THE GUIDE

This guide gives a detailed introduction to many of the world's most important and interesting shark species. The descriptions of the sharks are supported by illustrations that show the form, coloration, and markings of the given species. Information is also provided on the method of reproduction used by the featured shark.

The guide is divided into eight color-coded sections represent the eight orders of shark. The colored banding across the to each entry indicates the order which the species belongs.

The common name of each shark, which is usually based on its physical appearance or its behavior, is followed by the scientific name.

This figure is related to the maximum size—male or female—ever measured.

LAMNIFORMES

Basking Shark

Cetorhinus maximus

Maximum length: 49¼ feet (15 m); few over 33 feet (10 m)

■ MAIN FEATURES
The basking shark is the second largest fish in the world; the largest is the whale shark. Its huge size makes it easy to identify, as do its very broad gill slits that extend around the top and bottom of the head. The grayish brown body is streamlined and stout, with a strong, crescent-shaped tail fin and lateral keels. The short snout is narrow and conical, with huge

jaws that ex
the shark fe
Basking
migratory,
specific lo
regional c
they are te
large live

■ FEED
Basking
visitors
tempera
advanta
coastal
large b
them c
slowly

Captions and labels draw attention to particular points of interest about the species.

BIG FISH
This is the second largest species of shark, and is occasionally killed for its oil (squalene), fins, skin, and meat.

The map is marked with a dark blue area to indicate the worldwide distribution of each species.

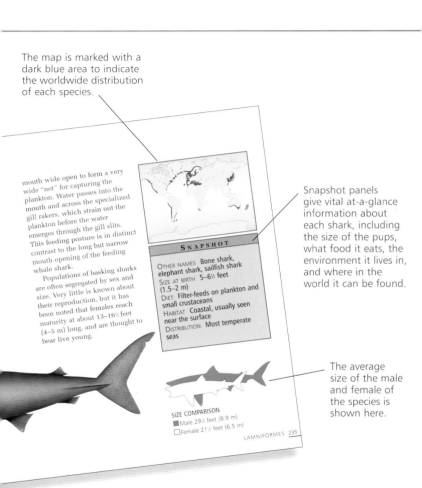

mouth wide open to form a very wide "net" for capturing the plankton. Water passes into the mouth and across the specialized gill rakers, which strain out the plankton before the water emerges through the gill slits. This feeding posture is in distinct contrast to the long but narrow mouth opening of the feeding whale shark.

Populations of basking sharks are often segregated by sex and size. Very little is known about their reproduction, but it has been noted that females reach maturity at about 13–16½ feet (4–5 m) long, and are thought to bear live young.

SNAPSHOT

OTHER NAMES Bone shark, elephant shark, sailfish shark
SIZE AT BIRTH 5–6½ feet (1.5–2 m)
DIET Filter-feeds on plankton and small crustaceans
HABITAT Coastal, usually seen near the surface
DISTRIBUTION Most temperate seas

Snapshot panels give vital at-a-glance information about each shark, including the size of the pups, what food it eats, the environment it lives in, and where in the world it can be found.

SIZE COMPARISON
■ Male 29¼ feet (8.9 m)
□ Female 21½ feet (6.5 m)

The average size of the male and female of the species is shown here.

Classifying Sharks

■ Naming Sharks *170*

SHARKS ARE GIVEN COMMON names to describe
their appearance. This can cause confusion—one
shark may end up with more than one name. To avoid
this problem, scientists have divided sharks into eight
orders, which have been further subdivided into
families, with a variable number of species in each.

Naming Sharks

The confusing variety of common names used for sharks can mean that two people may be talking about the same animal and not know it. As an example, *Carcharias taurus* is known as the gray nurse in Australia. In North America and New Zealand, it is referred to as the sand tiger. In South Africa it is the spotted raggedtooth shark. The variety of names given to this species seems to stem from its appearance and from media coverage of shark attacks. It is a fierce-looking shark, with long, protruding teeth and yellow eyes.

SCIENTIFIC NAMING

The value of scientific names is therefore to remove much of this confusion by providing an internationally recognized single name that not only defines a particular species but helps to place it in a standardized taxonomic position. Taxonomy (from the Greek words *tasso*, to arrange, and *nomia*, distribution) refers to the classification of organisms within related groups

DECEIVING LOOKS The sand tiger is also called the gray nurse and the ragged-tooth because of its fierce appearance.

...UE BOTHER The shortfin
...ko *Isurus oxyrinchus* (above)
...sometimes called the blue
...inter, causing confusion with
...e blue shark *Prionace glauca*.

...DER COVER The tope shark
...leorhinus galeus (right) is also
...own as the soupfin, vitamin,
...ool, and snapper shark.

...various sizes. Sharks belong to
...e phylum Chordata, the
...bphylum Vertebrata, the class
...ondricthyes, one of 8 orders,
... families, about 99 genera and
...proximately 488 species.
...cientists cautiously use words
...ke "approximately" and "about"

with these numbers; their
unwillingness to confirm numbers
is an indication of the dynamic
nature of taxonomy—new species,
and new discoveries about
familiar species, keep the classification of all organisms in a state
of flux.

The eight main groups, or orders, of sharks are based on common features, including body and snout shape, number of gill openings, position of mouth, and the presence or absence of anal fin and dorsal fin spines.

Order Hexanchiformes—the sixgill, sevengill, and frilled sharks—is a small group that is worldwide in distribution and occurs mostly in deep water.

Order Squaliformes—dogfish sharks—is a large, varied group found in all oceans, sometimes at great depths.

Order Pristiophoriformes—the sawsharks—is a minor group of harmless bottom sharks that resemble small sawfishes.

Order Squatiniformes—the angelsharks—is a distinctive group comprising a single family of at least 15 species.

Order Heterodontiformes—the bullhead sharks—are the only living sharks that combine fin spines on their two dorsal fins and an anal fin.

Order Orectolobiformes—the carpetsharks—is a small but diverse group of warm-water sharks with uniquely formed barbels just inside the nostrils.

Order Lamniformes—the mackerel sharks—are found in all seas except for high Arctic and Antarctic latitudes.

Order Carcharhiniformes—the groundsharks—dominates the world's shark fauna. Most of the potentially dangerous species occur in this group.

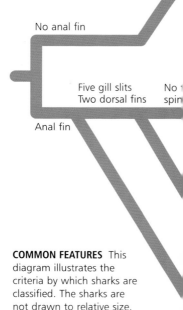

No anal fin

Five gill slits
Two dorsal fins

No †
spin

Anal fin

COMMON FEATURES This diagram illustrates the criteria by which sharks are classified. The sharks are not drawn to relative size.

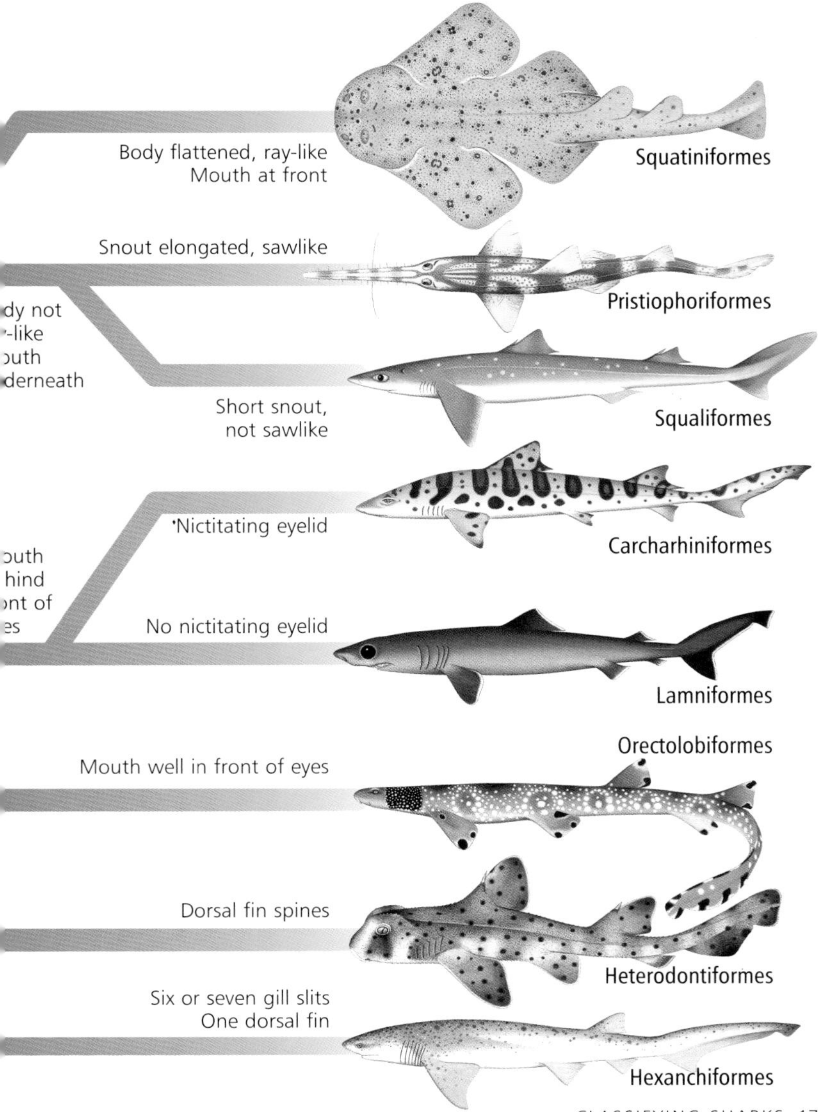

Body flattened, ray-like
Mouth at front

Squatiniformes

Snout elongated, sawlike

Pristiophoriformes

dy not
-like
outh
derneath

Short snout,
not sawlike

Squaliformes

Nictitating eyelid

Carcharhiniformes

outh
hind
ont of
es

No nictitating eyelid

Lamniformes

Mouth well in front of eyes

Orectolobiformes

Dorsal fin spines

Heterodontiformes

Six or seven gill slits
One dorsal fin

Hexanchiformes

The order Hexanchiformes comprises two families—frilled, and sixgill and sevengill sharks. The sharks have six or seven pairs of gill openings (most sharks have five), an anal fin, and a single, spineless, dorsal fin. They are wide-ranging and occur in deep and shallow water. Frilled sharks (family Chlamydoselachidae) have compressed, eel-like bodies.

The mouth is at the tip of the snout rather than under the head, and they have teeth with three cusps in both jaws. The sixgill and sevengill sharks (family Hexanchidae), also known as cow sharks and bull sharks, have fairl cylindrical bodies, mouths under the head, and large, comblike teeth in the lower jaw. There are five species.

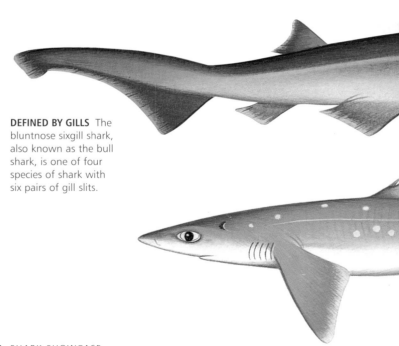

DEFINED BY GILLS The bluntnose sixgill shark, also known as the bull shark, is one of four species of shark with six pairs of gill slits.

The seven families in the order Squaliformes (dogfish sharks) have two dorsal fins (mostly spined), no anal fin, a short to moderately long conical snout, and five pairs of gill openings. Most occur in deep water on the slopes of continents and islands, but some occur in temperate inshore waters, and a few in the Arctic and Antarctic.

Family traits Bramble sharks (family Echinorhinidae) are large and cylindrical with small, spineless dorsal fins on the back, over the pelvic fins. Dogfish sharks (family Squalidae) and gulper sharks (family Centrophoridae) are moderate-sized and cylindrical. The lanternsharks (family Etmopteridae) are small to dwarf cylindrical sharks with grooved spines on the dorsal fins. Sleeper sharks (family Somniosidae) are moderate-sized to gigantic cylindrical sharks. Roughsharks (family Oxynotidae) are unusual-looking deep-water sharks. Kitefin sharks (family Dalatiidae) are dwarf to moderate-sized cylindrical or slightly compressed sharks with broad dorsal fins.

AGE OLD The spiny dogfish is the most common species of shark in the world. It is extremely slow-growing and lives for up to 70 years.

■ Sawsharks, belonging to the order Pristiophoriformes, have one family (Pristiophoridae), comprising five species. They are small to moderate-sized, elongated, flat-headed sharks believed to be the closest living relatives of the rays.

Sawsharks have large pectoral fins, two spineless dorsal fins, and no anal fin. The shark's head, which has five pairs of gill openings, is depressed, with a distinctive, long, flattened snout that comprises up to 30 percent of the shark's total length. As the shark's name implies, the snout resembles a saw, with teeth on the edges and two barbels mid-way. The snout is probably used to disable the prey.

The skin of the sawshark is san to grayish brown with irregular brown splotches. Generally the underside is pale and the snout a pinkish color. The body is covered in tiny denticles, and t dorsal and pectoral fins are sca

The species is ovoviviparous livebearing, which means that t young emerge from egg capsule within the body. They deliver between 3 and 22 pups per litte The pups are born with the teet of the saw folded back against t blade, so the mother is less like to be injured during the birth.

Sawsharks occur mainly in shallow water on the shelves and upper slopes of the North Atlantic, Indian, Southern, and Pacific oceans.

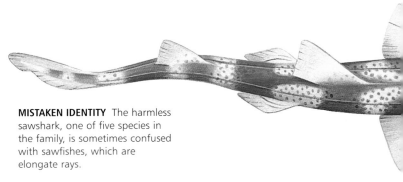

MISTAKEN IDENTITY The harmless sawshark, one of five species in the family, is sometimes confused with sawfishes, which are elongate rays.

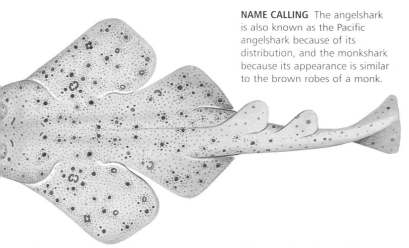

Angelsharks, which belong to the order Squatiniformes, comprise a single family (Squatinidae) of sharks. While ray-like in appearance—the eyes are located on top of the head—angelsharks are only distantly related to the rays. They have two small, spineless dorsal fins; no anal fin; a short, truncated snout with a mouth at the tip; five pairs of gill openings; and huge pectoral fins with angular extensions covering the gill openings.

Most of the more than 15 species of angelshark occur inshore in temperate waters, with a few found in deep tropical waters. They are largely nocturnal, and tend to be sluggish. Ovoviviparous livebearers, they give birth to between 8 and 13 pups per litter. The larger the female, the larger the litter.

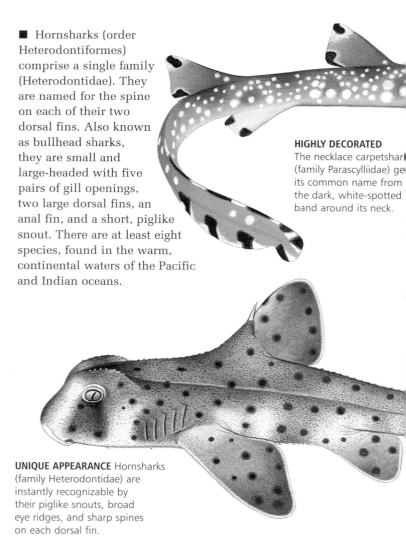

■ Hornsharks (order Heterodontiformes) comprise a single family (Heterodontidae). They are named for the spine on each of their two dorsal fins. Also known as bullhead sharks, they are small and large-headed with five pairs of gill openings, two large dorsal fins, an anal fin, and a short, piglike snout. There are at least eight species, found in the warm, continental waters of the Pacific and Indian oceans.

HIGHLY DECORATED
The necklace carpetshark (family Parascylliidae) gets its common name from the dark, white-spotted band around its neck.

UNIQUE APPEARANCE Hornsharks (family Heterodontidae) are instantly recognizable by their piglike snouts, broad eye ridges, and sharp spines on each dorsal fin.

The order Orectolobiformes comprises seven families of small to gigantic sharks. They have two spineless dorsal fins, an anal fin, a short mouth in front of the eyes, five pairs of gill openings, and nostrils with barbels. The pectoral fins of many species are specially adapted for "walking" on the sea floor. They are found in warm-temperate and tropical waters, with most species occurring in the Indo-West Pacific.

At least six species of the collared carpetshark (family Parascylliidae) have been described. They are all small, narrow-headed, long-tailed, and slender. The so-called blind sharks (family Brachaeluridae)—named for the fact that they close their eyes when caught by anglers—are small, stocky, broad-headed, long-tailed sharks. The wobbegong sharks (family Orectolobidae) are small to large with flat, broad bodies and short tails. There are at least 12 species of longtailed carpetshark (family Hemiscylliidae), divided into the epaulette and bamboo sharks. The single species of zebra shark (family Stegostomatidae) is large, stocky, and broad-headed. The broad-headed nurse sharks (family Ginglymostomatidae) are small to large and stocky. The single species of whale shark (family Rhincodontidae) is the largest living fish. These sharks are gigantic and broad-headed.

■ The eight families of ground shark (order Carcharhiniformes) range from small to very large. They have two spineless dorsal fins, an anal fin, a short mouth in front of the eyes, five pairs of gill openings, nictitating eyelids, and nostrils that usually lack barbels. These are the dominant sharks both in abundance and in number of species.

Family traits Catsharks (family Scyliorhinidae) are the largest of all shark families, with over 102 species. Finback catsharks (family Proscylliidae) have comblike teeth at the corners. The false catsharks (family Pseudotriakidae) have deep grooves in front of their eyes. The barbeled houndsharks (family Leptochariidae) are small and tapering, with barbels on the nostrils. Houndsharks (family Triakidae) are slender, with an arched or angular mouth. Weasel sharks (family Hemigaleidae) have nearly circular eyes. Requiem sharks (family Carcharhinidae), are a diverse group with more than 50 species. Hammerhead sharks (family Sphyrnidae) have the distinctive hammer-shaped head with eyes at extreme ends.

ONE IDENTITY Like the leopard shark, the crocodile shark has no other common names.

SPOTS AND STRIPES The leopard shark has no other common names, though it is often mistaken for the dangerous tiger shark.

The order Lamniformes ontains seven families of ostly large sharks. They have vo spineless dorsal fins, an anal ı, five pairs of gill openings, ıd a long mouth extending ıst the eyes.

ımily traits Goblin sharks ımily Mitsukurinidae) are ysterious deep-water sharks. ınd tiger sharks (family lontaspididae) are large and out-bodied. Crocodile sharks (family Pseudocarchariidae) are small, long, cylindrical sharks with short, conical snouts. The single species of megamouth shark (family Megachasmidae) is a very large, deep-water filter-feeder. Its huge mouth appears at the end of its very short, broadly rounded snout. Thresher sharks (family Alopiidae) are large, stout-bodied sharks with large pectoral fins, big eyes, and an enormous caudal fin, which is almost as long as the rest of the body. There are three or four species. Basking sharks (family Cetorhinidae) are gigantic, stocky filter-feeders with massive gill openings. The mackerel sharks (family Lamnidae) are large to very large, spindle-shaped sharks with distinct, broad gill openings. There are five species.

Hexanchiformes

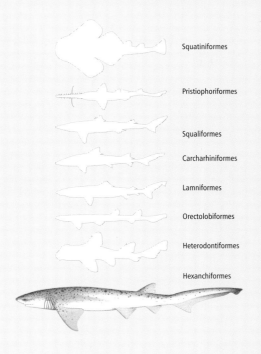

Squatiniformes

Pristiophoriformes

Squaliformes

Carcharhiniformes

Lamniformes

Orectolobiformes

Heterodontiformes

Hexanchiformes

SHARKS WITH A SINGLE dorsal fin, six or seven pairs of gill openings, and an anal fin belong to the order Hexanchiformes. This small group contains two families and at least five species, is worldwide in distribution, and occurs mostly in deep water.

Bluntnose Sixgill Shark

Hexanchus griseus

Maximum length: 15¾ feet (4.8 m)

■ MAIN FEATURES

The bluntnose sixgill shark has a massive body, with a long and powerful tail, which it uses to swim in a strong, constant motion. A single dorsal fin is located to the rear of the body, slightly in front of the anal fin below. The eyes are small, and set on the side of the wide, short-snouted head. The shark has six pairs of gill slits.

Only two other shark species have six gill slits: the frilled sha[rk] and the bigeyed sixgill shark *Hexanchus vitulus*. The latter belongs to the same family as the bluntnose sixgill shark, and can be distinguished by its slender body and large eyes. It has five rows of sawlike teeth on each side of its lower jaw, whereas the bluntnose sixgill shark has six rows of similar teeth.

The upper jaw of the bluntnose sixgill shark has smaller recurved teeth with a single cusp. It is a large shark and a voracious predator of other large fishes, such as sharks, billfishes, dolphin, cod, and flounder,

COMMERCIAL PRODUCT
The bluntnose sixgill shark is fished in many parts of the world for both its meat and its oil.

hich it can quickly cut into bite-
zed chunks with its teeth. It also
kes smaller prey, such as squid,
rring, crab, and shrimp.

LOCATION
ie bluntnose sixgill shark is
und both near the bottom
d in the water column above
and and continental shelves,
curring mainly at depths of
0–5,400 feet (200–1,800 m). It
nds to prefer dimly lit or dark
aters, and is seen at night near
e surface of the open ocean.
nall sixgills move close inshore
d forage near the bottom, but in
astal waters adults usually stay
low 330 feet (100 m).

SNAPSHOT

OTHER NAMES Sixgill, bull shark
SIZE AT BIRTH 24–28 inches
(60–70 cm)
DIET Wide-ranging, including
other sharks, rays, bottom fishes,
and even crabs and seals
HABITAT Shelves and slopes
from the surface to 5,400 feet
(1,800 m)
DISTRIBUTION Coastal, worldwide
including oceanic islands

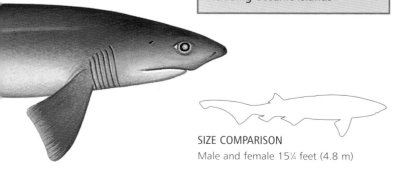

SIZE COMPARISON
Male and female 15¼ feet (4.8 m)

Broadnose Sevengill Shark

Notorynchus cepedianus

Maximum length: 10 feet (3 m)

■ MAIN FEATURES

The broadnose sevengill shark is immediately recognizable because of its seven pairs of gill slits—most shark species have only five pairs. Its other unusual feature is a single, small dorsal fin. It has a wide head with a short, blunt snout and small eyes. It is a large and powerful shark. Its silvery gray to brownish back and sides are speckled with numerous small dark and white spots, while the underside is pale. The juvenile sharks have white margins on their rear fins.

The teeth of the broadnose sevengill shark are very effectiv for cutting. The teeth of the upp jaw are jagged with cusps, exce for a single middle tooth; the teeth of the bottom jaw are com shaped. The shark's diet includ other sharks, rays, bony fishes, seals, and carrion. It bites piece of flesh from other sharks caugh by gill nets and hooks.

Males mature at about 5 feet (1.5 m), and females at about 6 feet (1.8 m). They bear live young in shallow bays. Litter sizes vary, and can be as large a 82 pups. The pups are born at about 16–18 inches (40–45 cm).

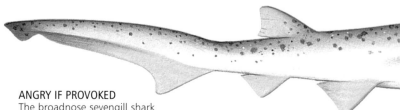

ANGRY IF PROVOKED
The broadnose sevengill shark has not been known to attack humans in the wild, but may be dangerous to incautious handlers.

LOCATION

The broadnose sevengill shark lives in temperate waters on continental shelves, at depths down to 450 feet (135 m). The species is widespread, although it is not particularly abundant. It will often come close inshore in shallow bays and inlets, but does not rest on the seabed. This might explain why it is not commonly seen by divers.

There are no records of broadnose sevengill sharks attacking people in the wild, but it is known that they will scavenge on human corpses. They are extremely aggressive when provoked and will struggle vigorously to escape when captured.

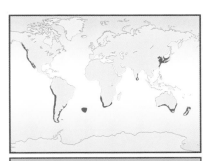

SNAPSHOT

OTHER NAMES Cowshark, groundshark
SIZE AT BIRTH 16–18 inches (40–45 cm)
DIET Wide-ranging, including other sharks, rays, and seals
HABITAT Shallow bays and estuaries along the continental shelf to 450 feet (135 m)
DISTRIBUTION Temperate coastal, except for northern Atlantic

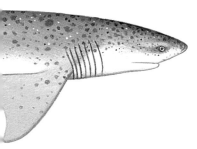

SIZE COMPARISON
■ Male 8 feet (2.4 m)
☐ Female 6¼ feet (1.9 m)

Frilled Shark

Chlamydoselachus anguineus

Maximum length: 6½ feet (2 m)

■ MAIN FEATURES

The frilled shark, or eel shark, has a long, slender body with an elongate tail fin, which gives it an almost eel-like appearance and one of its common names. A single, small dorsal fin is located well back on its dark chocolate-brown body, directly above the large anal fin.

The pectoral fins are short and rounded. This shark has six pairs of large gill slits—most sharks have five—the first pair of which joins under the throat. The gills are surrounded by frilly margins of skin—hence the common name of frilled shark. Its snout is short, while the lower jaw is long, with the mouth almost at the tip of the snout rather than under the head. The frilled shark's teeth have broad bases with three sharp cusps separated by two small intermediate cusps. Not much is known about its diet, but with such teeth, it is assumed that it feeds on small deep-water fishes and squid.

Female frilled sharks bear 8 to 12 live young, about 16 inches (40 cm) long. Gestation is thought to be one to two years. The evolution of the frilled shark is the subject of some debate.

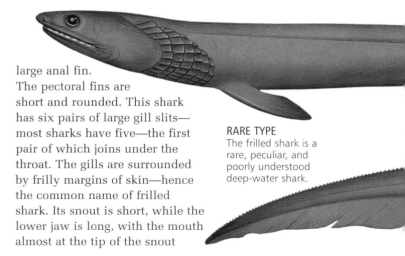

RARE TYPE
The frilled shark is a rare, peculiar, and poorly understood deep-water shark.

LOCATION

[Ge]nerally, very little is known [ab]out the biology and ecology of [th]is shark, the only living member [of] the frilled shark family. It is [fo]und on the bottom shelves and [up]per slopes around continents [an]d large islands. Occasionally, it [is] seen near the surface in open [w]aters, but it usually lives at a [de]pth of up to 4,200 feet (1,280 m), [so] the only chance of observing it [is] from a deep-water submersible. [It] is sometimes collected as [by]-catch during bottom trawling.

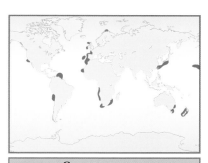

SNAPSHOT	

OTHER NAMES Frill-gilled shark, eel shark

SIZE AT BIRTH 16 inches (40 cm)

DIET Other sharks, squid, fishes

HABITAT Benthic, on the continental slopes and island margins, usually at depths of 400–4,200 feet (120–1,280 m)

DISTRIBUTION Wide-ranging but patchy in all oceans except northwestern Atlantic coast

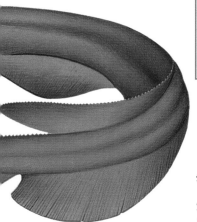

SIZE COMPARISON
Male and female 6½ feet (2 m)

Squaliformes

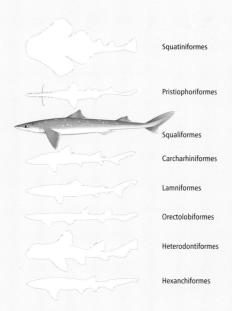

Squatiniformes

Pristiophoriformes

Squaliformes

Carcharhiniformes

Lamniformes

Orectolobiformes

Heterodontiformes

Hexanchiformes

THE ORDER SQUALIFORMES comprises sharks
with two dorsal fins (mostly with spines), no anal fin,
cylindrical bodies, short mouths, and snouts. Many
have powerful cutting teeth in both jaws. This large
and varied group contains seven families and
more than 94 species.

Blackbelly Lantern Shark

Etmopterus lucifer

Maximum length: 18 inches (45 cm)

■ MAIN FEATURES

This small, stocky shark has spines in front of each dorsal fin. Its dorsal side and flanks are brownish, the underbody black, and there is no anal fin. It has bladelike teeth and feeds on squid, lanternfish, and hard-shelled crustaceans.

A variety of physical features distinguish the blackbelly lanternsharks from the other lanternsharks. These include the arrangement and number of the denticles, and subtle differences in fin size and coloration. It is closely related to *Etmopterus perryi*, the dwarf dogshark, which is a mere 8 inches (20 cm) long, and is probably the smallest living shark.

The blackbelly lanternshark, which is widespread on outer continental shelves, lives on or near the bottom at depths of up to 3,300 feet (1,000 m). Its mode of reproduction, given that not much is known about these sharks, is presumed to be ovoviviparous livebearing, like most sharks.

SELF-LIGHTING
Lantern sharks produce their own light, whereas other fishes rely on a symbiotic relationship with certain bacteria.

oluminescence All of the 17 or
re species of the group known
lanternsharks have numerous,
nute, bioluminescent (light-
oducing) photophores along the
derside of their bodies. The
ht from the photophores is a
ans of camouflage because it
ounter-illuminates" the shark.
The shark produces just
ough weak light on the
derside of its body to equal
e amount of down-welling
ht between it and the ocean's
rface. The effect of this optical
usion is that the shark merges
th the ocean and cannot be
en by potential predators, nor
its unsuspecting prey.

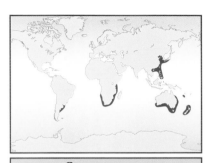

SNAPSHOT

OTHER NAMES **Lucifer shark**
SIZE AT BIRTH **6 inches (15 cm)**
DIET **Squid, shrimp, small fishes**
HABITAT **Along slopes and
shelves at depths of
590–3,300 feet (180–1,000 m)**
DISTRIBUTION **Southern and
eastern Australia, New Zealand,
and the China Sea**

SIZE COMPARISON
■ Male 13¾ inches (35 cm)
☐ Female 13½ inches (34 cm)

Bramble Shark

Echinorhinus brucus

Maximum length: 8½ feet (2.6 m)

■ MAIN FEATURES

The bramble shark is a spiny-skinned dogfish, one of two species of the bramble shark family. The bodies of both species are short and stout, the heads slightly flattened. There is a small spiracle behind each eye and in front of the first of five pairs of gill slits. Two spineless dorsal fins are located well back on the body above the pelvic fins. Anal fins are absent.

The shark is grayish brown with white around the mouth and underneath the snout, and black along its relatively large f margins. Denticles, usually abo ⅜ inch (15 mm) wide at the bas cover its body.

Little is known about the ecology and habits of this shark It appears to be primarily a dee water species, dwelling in cold temperate to tropical seas on continental and island shelves and upper slopes at depths of 1,300–3,000 feet (400–900 m). Individuals are seen occasional in more shallow waters.

This slow-moving species is probably a suction-feeder of cra and cephalopods near the botto of the ocean floor. It also takes fishes such as juvenile sixgill sharks, flatfishes, and herring.

SPEEDY SURPRISE
Although they are sluggish, bramble sharks are capable of surprising speed in short bursts.

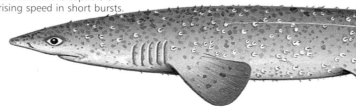

emales are mature at about 7 feet
.1 m) long. They bear up to 24
ve young.

DIFFERENT SPECIES

he other species of bramble
ark, *Echinorhinus cookei*,
nown as the prickly shark, has
uch smaller and less prominent
pinelike denticles, which are
out ⅕ inch (5 mm) in diameter
their base. They are scattered
ver the shark's body as well as
the underside of the snout in
dults, and are sometimes fused
to plates. This shark is brown
dark gray above, with a lighter
elly. It is most commonly
ncountered in the Mediterranean
ea and along the west coast of
urope and Africa.

SNAPSHOT

OTHER NAMES Spinous shark
SIZE AT BIRTH Unknown
DIET Smaller sharks, bony fishes,
and crabs
HABITAT Continental shelves and
upper slopes from 1,300–3,000
feet (400–900 m)
DISTRIBUTION Western Atlantic,
Argentina, eastern Atlantic, India,
New Zealand, southern Australia

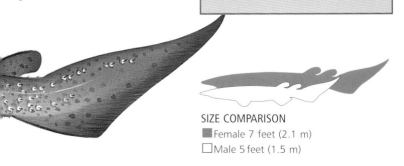

SIZE COMPARISON
■ Female 7 feet (2.1 m)
□ Male 5 feet (1.5 m)

Cookiecutter Shark

Isistius brasiliensis

Maximum length: 20 inches (50 cm)

■ MAIN FEATURES

Before its feeding behavior was discovered, this species was known as the "cigar shark." It is a small, brown shark with a short snout. Its cigar-like appearance is enhanced by its small dorsal fins being displaced to the rear of its body, its nearly symmetrical caudal fin, and by the lack of an anal fin. It also has a black collar around the back of its head.

The cookiecutter shark and its close relative, the largetooth cookiecutter shark *Isistius plutodus*, have specialized suctorial jaws and lips, and razor-sharp, sawlike, lower teeth. The shark forms a suction cap with its lips on the skin of its prey, then bites and swivels around to cut out an oval-shape plug of tissue, acting just as a cookiecutter does in pastry.

The cookiecutter shark's victims include large marlins, tunas, seals, whales, and dolphins, and it has even bitten the rubberized dome of a nuclear submarine. Scientists believe that it uses its bioluminescent light organs, which glow luminous

INDISCRIMINATE ATTACKER
The highly predatory cookiecutter shark has been known to attack a nuclear submarine.

een in the dark, to lure fast-
swimming prey close, so that it
can ambush them.

LOCATION

tropical shark, it has been
caught at the surface at night, but
normally inhabits depths as
great as 11,500 feet (3,570 m). It is
ovoviviparous, but nothing is
known about the size of its litters.

The deep waters of the open
ocean are home to many such
small, predatory sharks. These
sharks have developed special
features and behaviors that make
it possible for them to prey on the
many organisms that live in their
habitat, and thus survive in dim
or dark waters.

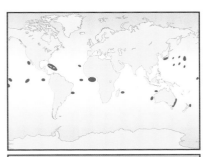

SNAPSHOT

OTHER NAMES Cigar shark
SIZE AT BIRTH Unknown
DIET Squid, and pieces of large
fishes and marine mammals
HABITAT Oceanic, migrating from
depths of 11,500 feet (3,570 m)
to the surface each night
DISTRIBUTION Widespread, mostly
oceanic

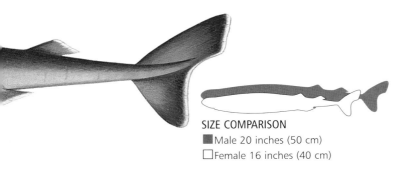

SIZE COMPARISON
■ Male 20 inches (50 cm)
□ Female 16 inches (40 cm)

Greenland Sleeper Shark

Somniosus microcephalus

Maximum length: 21 feet (6.4 m)

■ MAIN FEATURES

The Greenland shark is a gigantic dogfish—the only polar shark of the Atlantic. It lives in deep water to 1,800 feet (550 m) at temperatures of 36–45°F (2–7°C), only coming up to shallow water during the colder months. At such temperatures, it is generally not encountered by divers, although occasionally it may be caught by fishers. The Greenland sleeper tends to be a sluggish beast, and is known to provide little resistance when captured. Nevertheless, like all sharks, it should always be handled carefully.

There are four or five species of sleeper shark. All have a short and rounded snout, a caudal fin with a well-developed lower lobe and two small, spineless dorsal fins. They lack an anal fin. Greenland sleeper sharks vary in color. Some are mottled, while others range from pinkish to brown, black, or purplish gray.

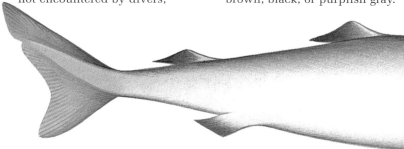

SECRET WEAPON
This sluggish shark can capture wily and fast-moving creatures, possibly because of brightly luminescent copepods that attach themselves to the corneas of the shark's eyes and attract such prey.

FEEDING AND BREEDING

The teeth of the Greenland shark's upper jaw are long and pointed, very different from those of its lower jaw, which are strongly oblique, sharp, and close set. These teeth allow it to gouge large chunks of flesh from dead whales, and probably to remove the heads of seals and sea lions rapidly before dining on the carcasses. It also eats fishes such as salmon, and a variety of bottom-dwelling fishes.

Little is known about the Greenland shark's reproductive behavior. It was recently discovered to be ovoviviparous, bearing about 10 pups, 15 inches (38 cm) long, in each litter.

SNAPSHOT

OTHER NAMES Sleeper shark, gurry shark
SIZE AT BIRTH 15 inches (38 cm)
DIET Seals, bottom fishes, invertebrates, and carrion
HABITAT From shallow water to 1,800 feet (550 m)
DISTRIBUTION North Atlantic Ocean

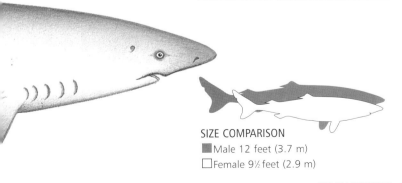

SIZE COMPARISON
■ Male 12 feet (3.7 m)
☐ Female 9½ feet (2.9 m)

Spiny Dogfish

Squalus acanthias

Maximum length: 5 feet (1.5 m)

■ MAIN FEATURES

The spiny dogfish is also known as the piked dogfish or whitespotted spurdog. It is identified by a large spiracle behind each large eye, the presence of spines on the two dorsal fins, and the lack of an anal fin. It ranges from gray to brown in color, with small, white spots above a light underside. Spiny dogfish are cold-water sharks, preferring temperatures from 45–59°F (7–15°C). They are caught in waters down to about 2,600 feet (800 m) deep, but not exclusively in deep water. They form extremely large schools, routinely frequenting the shallow and coastal waters of higher latitudes in spring and fall, and migrating into deep waters during the cooler winter months.

The spiny dogfish is of high commercial importance in many parts of the world. However, with its slow growth rate and low fecundity, it is very susceptible to overfishing, and has been overharvested in many regions.

COMMERCIAL PROPERTY
While still probably the world's most abundant shark, this long-lived (to 70 years), bottom-dwelling species is severely depleted due to overfishing.

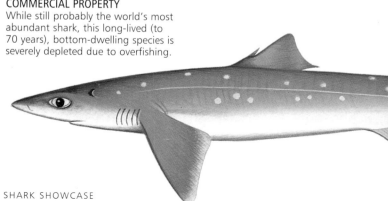

FEEDING AND BREEDING
Many sharks from the dogfish family (Squalidae) ascend at dusk and return at dawn to the safety of the deep midwaters, relying on their large eyes and good vision in low light to detect prey. The diet includes small fishes, such as cod, herring, menhaden, and haddock, as well as invertebrates such as krill, squid, scallops, and crustaceans.

This species is extremely slow-growing and lives for up to 70 years. Females reach sexual maturity at 21–25 years old. They give birth to up to 20 live young, about 8–12 inches (20–30 cm) long, after a gestation of 18–24 months.

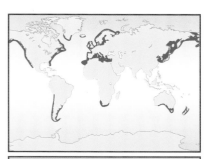

S N A P S H O T

OTHER NAMES Piked dogfish, skittledog, white-spotted dogfish, spotted spiny dogfish, spurdog
SIZE AT BIRTH 8–12 inches (20–30 cm)
DIET Small fishes, krill, and squid
HABITAT Coastal, from shallow water to 2,600 feet (800 m)
DISTRIBUTION Atlantic and Pacific oceans; southeast Australia; New Zealand; tip of Africa

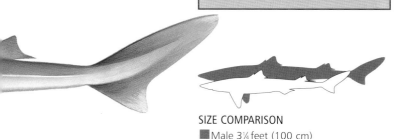

SIZE COMPARISON
■ Male 3¼ feet (100 cm)
□ Female 2½ feet (80 cm)

Prickly Dogfish

Oxynotus bruniensis

Maximum length: 2⅖ feet (73 cm)

■ MAIN FEATURES

Among the most unusual looking sharks of the deep ocean bottom are the roughsharks (Oxynotidae). These small sharks have a stout body that is laterally compressed and bears a prominent ridge on the abdomen. Most notable are the high, spined dorsal fins with their forward extensions, which give the appearance of two sails. There is no anal fin. The head is slightly flattened, with large eye prominent spiracles, and small gill slits. The nostrils are placed relatively close together and the fleshy mouth is small and usuall surrounded by labial furrows.

One of four roughshark species, the prickly dogfish is distinguished by its forward-pointing first dorsal spine and it skin, which is covered with rough, prickly denticles. The body is gray or brown with whitish

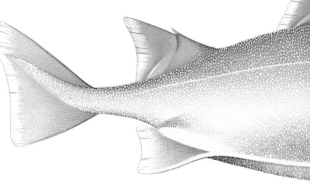

ODDLY UNIQUE
Very little is known about this curious benthic shark, one of only four species of roughshark.

argins on the tips of the dorsal s and trailing margins on the ctoral and pelvic fins.

The prickly dogfish occurs in mperate waters, dwelling at pths of about 165–1,640 feet)–500 m). Very little is known its biology. The diet consists of nthic invertebrates, such as gmented worms.

About seven young hatch from gs that are retained inside the other. The pups are born live at out 4 inches (10 cm) long.

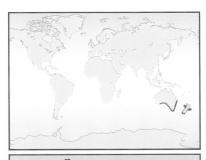

SNAPSHOT

OTHER NAMES **None**
SIZE AT BIRTH **4 inches (10 cm)**
DIET **Bottom invertebrates**
HABITAT **Temperate waters
165–1,640 feet (50–500 m) deep**
DISTRIBUTION **Southern Australia
and New Zealand**

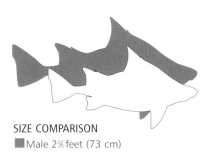

SIZE COMPARISON
■ Male 2⅖ feet (73 cm)
☐ Female 2 feet (60 cm)

Smallfin Gulper Dogfish

Centrophorus moluccensis

Maximum length: 39 inches (98 cm)

■ MAIN FEATURES

This slender, elegant deep-water shark has two dorsal fins with grooved spines (the second fin is small); elongated pectoral fins with pointed rear tips; and no anal fin. It has bladelike teeth in both jaws; a long, narrow snout; large, green eyes; and is covered in smooth, flat denticles. Coloring is light gray to gray-brown on the upper body and fins, and white on the underside. It has dusky or black blotches on the tips of the dorsal fins and upper lobe of the caudal fin.

The smallfin gulper shark is ovoviviparous, giving birth in summer to two pups per litter. It has a gestation period of at least one year. The young often have a pair of barbs on the dorsal fin spines, which resemble an arrow head, hence one of the gulper shark's common names.

Like other deep-water sharks in some areas, smallfin gulper numbers have decreased significantly due to overfishing.

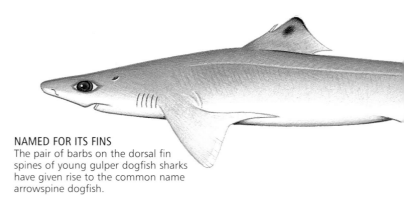

NAMED FOR ITS FINS
The pair of barbs on the dorsal fin spines of young gulper dogfish sharks have given rise to the common name arrowspine dogfish.

LOCATION

The soft bottoms of deep slopes, underwater ridges, and sea mounts support a range of deep-water sharks above a depth of about 6,550 feet (2,000 m). These include sleeper, lantern, frilled, goblin, sixgill, and sharpnose sevengill sharks, as well as catsharks and false catsharks. Relatively few species are found below these depths.

The smallfin gulper generally occurs in the Indo-West Pacific, though there are scattered records of sightings from the eastern coast of South Africa eastward to Australia and Japan.

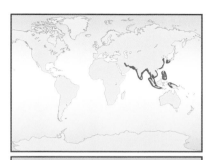

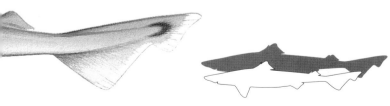

SIZE COMPARISON
■ Male 39 inches (98 cm)
☐ Female 34 inches (80 cm)

Spined Pygmy Shark

Squaliolus laticaudus

Maximum length: 10 inches (25 cm)

■ MAIN FEATURES

This deep-water dogfish rivals the dwarf dogfish *Etmopterus perryi* for the title of the smallest shark in the world. At the moment, not enough specimens have been collected to make a final decision. The spined pygmy and its Australian relative, the smalleye pygmy shark *Squaliolus aliae*, are unique in having a spine in front of the first dorsal fin but not the second. They are cigar-shaped, with a bulbous snout and a large spiracle behind the eye. The teeth of their upper jaw are small and narrow; the lower teeth tend to be larger and more bladelike.

On the undersides of their bodies, the spined pygmy sharks have many luminous photophores, which may help the shark blend in with weak illumination from the surface when viewed from below. This bioluminescence serves to camouflage these tiny sharks from predators, as it does for many deep-water sharks.

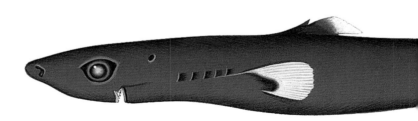

TINY TOT
This harmless shark is one of the smallest species in the world.

FEEDING AND BREEDING

The spined pygmy dogfish shark lives in temperate and tropical waters, offshore near continental and island land-masses. Like other deep-water sharks, it makes a daily migration to feed. It ascends at dusk and feeds during the night on squid, shrimp, and mid-water fishes, especially lanternfishes. It descends again at dawn. Unlike other species, it stops within 650 feet (200 m) of the surface, before heading down to ocean depths as great as 6,500 feet (2,000 m).

Little is known about the reproductive biology of the spined pygmy shark, but it is likely to be ovoviviparous.

SNAPSHOT

OTHER NAMES Dwarf shark, mid-water shark

SIZE AT BIRTH Less than ½ inch (12 mm)

DIET Squid, shrimp, and mid-water fishes

HABITAT Offshore, at depths of 650–6,500 feet (200–2,000 m)

DISTRIBUTION All oceans

SIZE COMPARISON
■ Male 8 inches (20 cm)
☐ Female 7 inches (18 cm)

Pristiophoriformes, Squatiniformes, Heterodontiformes

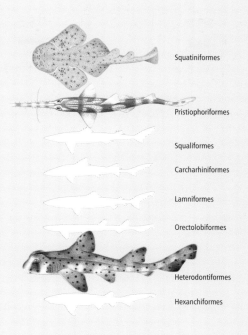

Squatiniformes

Pristiophoriformes

Squaliformes

Carcharhiniformes

Lamniformes

Orectolobiformes

Heterodontiformes

Hexanchiformes

PRISTIOPHORIFORMES IS A MINOR group of harmless
bottom sharks that resemble small sawfishes. The
order Squatiniformes is a highly distinctive group
of sharks comprising a single family of at least
15 species. Heterodontiformes are the only living
sharks that combine fin spines on their
two dorsal fins and an anal fin.

Common Sawshark

Pristiophorus cirratus

Maximum length: 4½ feet (1.4 m)

■ MAIN FEATURES

The common sawshark is endemic to southern Australia. Like all the sawshark family, it is immediately recognizable from its sawlike snout with a pair of barbels. Because of this snout, it can sometimes be confused with sawfishes. However, the shark's five pairs of gills are on the side of its head, while the sawfish's gills are underneath. Nor does the sawfish have a pair of barbels.

The common sawshark is a slender shark with a slightly depressed and flattened body. I has an attractive patterning of darker bands and brownish spo and blotches on a pale yellowis brown background. This shark i found only in temperate waters southern Australia.

The southern, or shortnose, sawshark *Pristiophorus nudipir nis*, also endemic to Australia, i found in a similar area. This brownish-gray shark prefers to dwell on the inner continental shelf to depths of 230 feet (90 m the common sawshark seems to prefer deeper water, occurring mostly on continental shelves and slopes to depths of about 1,000 feet (300 m).

CONFUSED LOOK
The harmless sawshark, one of five species in the family, is sometimes confused with sawfishes, which are elongate rays.

FEEDING AND BREEDING

[Sa]wsharks are often found lying [on] the sandy bottoms. They feed [by] trailing their barbels along the [bo]ttom to locate the small bony [fis]h that they eat. The teeth on [th]e snout are probably then used [fo]r stirring up sediment to rouse [th]e prey and strike it.

The common sawshark lives [fo]r more than 15 years. Like all [sa]wsharks, it is ovoviviparous. [M]ature females appear to breed [ev]ery one to two years, carrying [fro]m 3 to 22 young, with about [10] pups being the average. After [ab]out 12 months' gestation, the [pu]ps are born in shallow coastal [ar]eas. They are approximately [11]–15 inches (27–38 cm) long at [th]e time of birth.

SNAPSHOT

OTHER NAMES **Longnose sawshark**
SIZE AT BIRTH **11–15 inches (27–38 cm)**
DIET **Small bony fishes**
HABITAT **Continental shelves and slopes to about 1,000 feet (300 m)**
DISTRIBUTION **Southern Australia**

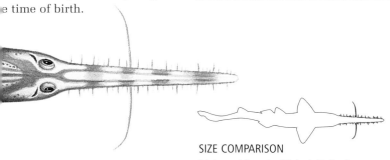

SIZE COMPARISON
Male and female 4½ feet (1.4 m)

Pacific Angelshark

Squatina californica

Maximum length: 5 feet (1.5 m)

■ MAIN FEATURES
Angelsharks are somewhat
unusual, flattened sharks that
are often mistaken for rays.
They used to be called monkfish
because the strange shape of their
heads resembles the hood on a
monk's cloak. The dozen species
range along temperate coasts from
shallow waters to more than
4,300 feet (1,310 m) deep. They
are unique in having a blunt nose;
the leading edge of their pectoral
fins is free from the body; and the
lower caudal fin lobe is longer
than the upper.

Males and females are mature
at about 3 feet (90 cm), and the
female is ovoviviparous, producing eggs that are retained within
her body. There are 8 to 13 pups
in each litter.

■ LOCATION
The Pacific angelshark is easily
identified by its large eyes,
a conspicuous spiracle, and
a generally brown-gray
coloration. During the day,
it remains

BUILT DIFFERENTLY
Ray-like in appearance, the largely
nocturnal Pacific angelshark is
flattened, with the edges of the
pectorals free from the body.

uried in sand on the bottom with ly its eyes and head exposed, ady to burst upward out of the nd and ambush a fish or squid ith its protruding, trap-like jaws d numerous spiky teeth.

Occasionally, divers may icounter a Pacific angelshark vimming over sandy bottoms ear kelp beds at depths of about) feet (3 m) and more. It can :come aggressive if harassed— diver or angler who foolishly abs the tail of an angelshark soon discovers how quickly the shark can bite and how painful the bite can be.

S N A P S H O T

OTHER NAMES **Monkshark**
SIZE AT BIRTH **16 inches (40 cm)**
DIET **An ambush predator, feeding on bottom fishes**
HABITAT **Coastal from shallow waters to 4,300 feet (1,310 m)**
DISTRIBUTION **Eastern Pacific, from southeastern Alaska to Baja California, and from Ecuador to southern Chile**

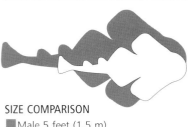

SIZE COMPARISON
▮ Male 5 feet (1.5 m)
☐ Female 3⅛ feet (95 cm)

California Hornshark

Heterodontus francisci

Maximum length: 4 feet (1.2 m), but rarely larger than 3 feet (1 m)

■ MAIN FEATURES

Named for the spine in front of each dorsal fin, the California hornshark is one of nine living species of the family known as bullhead, horn, or Port Jackson sharks. The sharks of this family are unmistakable, with their blunt foreheads, piglike snouts, and broad ridges over their eyes.

Their taxonomic name (from Greek for "mixed-tooth") refers the small, pointed teeth at the front of their jaw and blunt teeth at the rear.

California hornsharks are sandy- to gray-colored, and yellow on the underside, with small dark spots on their bodies and fins. They are very popular public aquariums. There, while sitting placidly on the bottom, they defy the commonly held belief that all sharks must swim in order to be able to breathe.

SEDENTARY TYPE
The hornshark is gener
sedentary and not
dangerous to humans
unless severely provoke
It can be encountered
and night, year-round
and is not uncommon

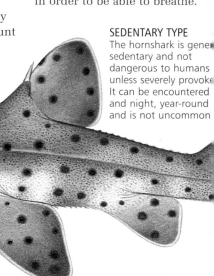

Feeding and breeding

The species is oviparous, laying two eggs a month for three months of the year. The mother carries the brown, corkscrew-shaped egg cases (always with a right-hand thread) in her mouth, before wedging them into crevices for protection. They hatch after seven to nine months, depending on water temperature. During the day, divers can find the sharks, as well as their egg cases, resting among large rocks in shallow-water kelp beds and at the base of boulders.

At night, the sharks patrol for food out in the open, eating the soft-bodied fish and crustaceans, sea urchins, and shellfish that live in the cool, shallow waters where these sharks occur.

SNAPSHOT

OTHER NAMES Bullhead shark, hornshark
SIZE AT BIRTH: 6 inches (15 cm)
DIET Sea urchins, crustaceans, and small fishes
HABITAT Among large rocks at the base of kelp beds
DISTRIBUTION Central California to Baja California

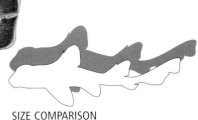

SIZE COMPARISON
■ Male 25 inches (64 cm)
☐ Female 23 inches (58 cm)

Orectolobiformes

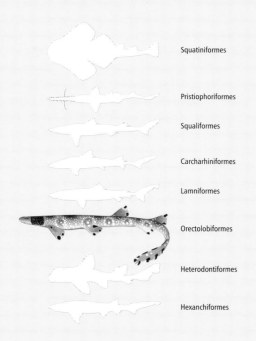

Squatiniformes

Pristiophoriformes

Squaliformes

Carcharhiniformes

Lamniformes

Orectolobiformes

Heterodontiformes

Hexanchiformes

THIS SMALL BUT DIVERSE GROUP of seven families
and at least 31 species of warm-water sharks
have piglike snouts and short mouths that in most
species are connected to the nostrils by grooves.
All are warm temperate or tropical sharks of
shallow to moderate depths.

Blind Shark

Brachaelurus waddi

Maximum length: 4 feet (1.2 m)

■ MAIN FEATURES
Blind sharks get their name from their habit of closing their eyes when caught by fishers. The blind shark, along with the blue-gray carpetshark *Brachaelurus colcloughi*, make up the blind shark family. They are closely related to nurse sharks, collared carpetsharks, and bamboosharks. Although often referred to as catsharks, they are actually related only distantly to them.

The blind shark has a stout, cylindrical, brown body, usually dotted with pale spots. Its two spineless dorsal fi are close together, with the first originating above the pelvic fins It has very large spiracles positioned behind and to the sid of the eyes. Its nostrils are particularly well developed, wit a pair of long, smooth nasal barbels, which are connected to the mouth by a groove that permits water that has passed over the olfactory organs to flow into the mouth.

The blind shark can essential be distinguished from the blue-gray carpetshark by the presence of a small (symphyseal) groove in the middle of the chin, which the blue-gray carpetshark lacks.

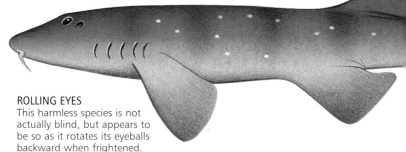

ROLLING EYES
This harmless species is not actually blind, but appears to be so as it rotates its eyeballs backward when frightened.

FEEDING AND BREEDING

This shark inhabits the more shallow, warm, temperate and tropical waters—it can occur in water just deep enough to cover It is also often found on the continental shelf to a depth of about 330 feet (100 m). During the day, the blind shark will shelter under ledges and in caves, and it commonly observed by divers under ledges but is rarely seen out in the open. It emerges after dark to forage on the reef and the adjacent sandy areas for cuttlefish, anemones, and crustaceans.

Females reach sexual maturity when about 26 inches (65 cm) long, and give birth during summer to as many as eight pups.

SNAPSHOT

OTHER NAMES **Brown catshark**
SIZE AT BIRTH **7 inches (18 cm)**
DIET **Reef fish and invertebrates**
HABITAT **Rocky shores from tide pools to 330 feet (100 m)**
DISTRIBUTION **Central eastern Australia**

SIZE COMPARISON
Male and female 4 feet (1.2 m)

Epaulette Shark

Hemiscyllium ocellatum

Maximum length: 3½ feet (90 cm)

■ MAIN FEATURES

The 13 species of longtailed carpetsharks are subdivided into the epaulette sharks (Hemiscyllium) and bamboosharks (Chiloscyllium). These usually small fish have thin, slightly flattened, elongated bodies. The two relatively

large, spineless dorsal fins are about the same size. The anal fin is far back on the underside, immediately in front of the caudal fin, from which it is separated by a notch. These short, stubby, paired fins are used by many species for "walking" across the bottom.

Most juvenile longtailed carpetsharks have broad and

contrasting bands of color on the body. In adult epaulette sharks these bands become spotted, and a prominent black spot develops above the pectoral fins. The yellowish or brownish body of *Hemiscyllium ocellatum* is covered with dark brown spots, and the characteristic large black spot has a white ring around it. Its nostrils and mouth are almost at the tip of the snout, which is short and rounded like that of all the epaulette sharks.

The solid bands of color of the juvenile carpetsharks fade or disappear altogether in adult bamboosharks such as the brownbanded bambooshark *Chiloscyllium punctatum*. It is a uniform brown as an adult. However, the adult slender

...mboo shark *Chiloscyllium ...dicum* is covered with small ...rk spots and bars, and has ...all side ridges. It has rounded ...rsal fins and the pointed snout ...pical of the bamboosharks.

Longtailed carpetsharks are ...mmon inshore on coral and ...cky reefs and in tide pools. ...vers often encounter adults, but ...veniles are rarely seen because ...ey hide within the reef. These ...cturnally active sharks feed ...ainly on small benthic ...vertebrates and fishes.

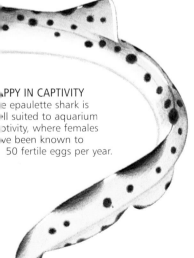

...PPY IN CAPTIVITY
...e epaulette shark is
...ll suited to aquarium
...otivity, where females
...ve been known to
... 50 fertile eggs per year.

SIZE COMPARISON
Male and female 3½ feet (107 cm)

Necklace Carpetshark

Parascyllium variolatum

Maximum length: 3 feet (90 cm)

■ MAIN FEATURES
With its long, slender, and slightly flattened body, and its long but almost indistinct tail, the necklace carpetshark has a quite eel-like appearance. It is easily identifiable by its dark gray-brown body scattered with numerous white spots and the large, black blotches on the edges of the fins. Most striking is the dark band, or collar, studded with small, bright, white spots that encircles the head like a necklace, hence its common name. It is also known as the varied carpetshark.

Its spiracles are small, and its nostrils bear short barbels (most probably for the purpose of chemosensory detection of prey) and grooves that are connected to the mouth.

Collared carpetsharks are closely related to nurse sharks and wobbegongs but are often mistaken for catsharks, which they resemble only superficially. The collared

GENERALLY SEDATE
The species is not considered dangerous but will bite if surprised or provoked. Numbers are declining as a result of overfishing.

rpetsharks are distinguished by e fact that their mouth is cated well in front of the eyes. e family has two genera: the rrhoscyllium, which have rbels on the throat; and the rascyllium, which do not.

FEEDING AND BREEDING
e necklace carpetshark is mmon on shallow, rocky reefs ong the southern temperate ast of Australia. It feeds and active at night, and is often countered by divers after dark. ring the day it is difficult to ot because it rests either in ves or on the bottom, where it

SNAPSHOT

OTHER NAMES Varied carpetshark, southern carpetshark, varied catshark
SIZE AT BIRTH Unknown
DIET Dentition would suggest benthic crustaceans
HABITAT Continental shelves to 1,600 feet (500 m)
DISTRIBUTION Southwestern and southern Australia

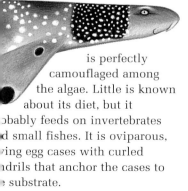

is perfectly camouflaged among the algae. Little is known about its diet, but it obably feeds on invertebrates d small fishes. It is oviparous, ving egg cases with curled drils that anchor the cases to e substrate.

SIZE COMPARISON
Male and female 3 feet (90 cm)

Nurse Shark

Ginglymostoma cirratum

Maximum length: 14 feet (4.3 m); rarely over 10 feet (3 m)

■ MAIN FEATURES

No one is sure how the nurse shark got its name, perhaps from the sucking noise made by a feeding nurse shark, which sounds like a nursing baby. This fairly large bottom dweller is uniformly brown to gray-brown and has large, rounded fins. Noticeable barbels protrude from the nasal openings in front of the corners of its small mouth. A small spiracle behind and below each eye allows it to take in water over the gills when breathing.

Common over inshore coral reefs in tropical waters, it is probably the shark that snorkelers and divers in the Caribbean see most often. Because they are abundant and easy to capture, handle, and transport, nurse sharks are common residents of public aquariums. Behaviorists have used them to study learning in sharks, and have been able to demonstrate that nurse sharks can be taught to react to novel situations.

QUIET TIME
The nurse shark does not need to swim to breathe, and can often be seen resting quietly on the ocean floor. It is not aggressive, unless provoked.

FEEDING AND BREEDING

Sluggish during the day, the nurse shark is active at night when it feeds on bottom-dwelling invertebrates, such as lobsters and other crustaceans, snails, clams, squid, octopus, and fishes slow enough to be caught by its gulping and inhaling style of feeding.

These ovoviviparous sharks conduct an interesting courtship. Male and female swim in close synchrony, the male alongside or slightly behind and below the female. (Sometimes, a second male accompanies them to stop the female from retreating.) When the male grabs the female's pectoral fin in his mouth, she rolls onto her back. He swims above her and inserts a clasper into her vent to deliver his sperm.

SNAPSHOT

OTHER NAMES **None**
SIZE AT BIRTH **11–12 inches
(27–30 cm)**
DIET **Benthic crustaceans, shellfish, octopus, and squid**
HABITAT **Shallow inshore reefs and mangroves to 40 feet (12 m)**
DISTRIBUTION **Western Atlantic, eastern Atlantic, eastern Pacific**

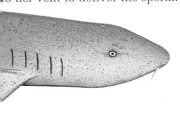

SIZE COMPARISON
■ Male 8¼ feet (2.5 m)
☐ Female 8 feet (2.4 m)

Ornate Wobbegong

Orectolobus ornatus

Maximum length: 9½ feet (2.9 m)

■ MAIN FEATURES

The ornate wobbegong has large, black-bordered, saddle-shaped markings on the back. The body is flattened and wide from the head to the back of the trunk, where it quickly tapers to the tail. On each side of the head there are five or six dermal lobes. Each nostril bears a single barbel and there is a groove from the back of each nostril to the mouth. The teeth are long and slender, well adapted for grasping prey such as small fishes.

This is one of four wobbegor species in the genus Orectolobu While the relative position of these wobbegongs' fins is simila to that of the tasselled wobbegong, the fin lobes in Orectolobus are smaller in comparison to the body. Orectolobus also differs in havi no dermal lobes or tassels on th chin or lower jaw. The back is smooth, which distinguishes sharks of this genus from the heavily tubercled cobbler wobbegong *Sutorectus tentaculatus*, common on the southwest coast of Australia.

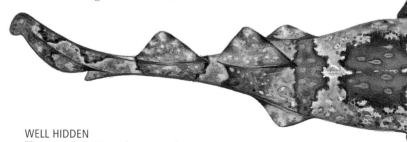

WELL HIDDEN
The ornately patterned, nocturnal banded wobbegong is brilliantly camouflaged on the ocean floor where it spends its days.

FEEDING AND BREEDING

he ornate wobbegong is a large, ommon inshore inhabitant of mperate rocky and tropical efs. During the day it rests in e open on rocky bottoms or ble coral, or it sometimes hides nder reef ledges. It becomes tive at night, searching the reef r invertebrates and fishes to eat. ivers should be cautious ecause this species can easily amouflage itself against the a floor, and it is considered ngerous—numerous provoked d unprovoked attacks have en documented. Females roduce litters of up to 12 pups, each about 8 inches (20 cm) long.

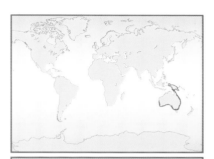

SIZE COMPARISON
Male and female 9½ feet (2.9 m)

Whale Shark

Rhincodon typus

Maximum length: 46 feet (14 m)

■ MAIN FEATURES

The sole living member of its family, the whale shark is the world's largest living fish. Its massive, fusiform body reaches lengths in excess of 46 feet (14 m). It has alternating thin, white, vertical bars and columns of spots on a dark background, with long ridges along the upper side of the body and a prominent lateral keel. The narrow mouth extends across the full width of its flattened head. The eyes are small and set far forward on the head. Each of its nostrils has a small barbel and the gill slits are long, extending above the pectoral fins. Above the relative small pelvic fins are the first of two dorsal fins. The powerful caudal fin is semicircular.

This shark is found in all tropical and subtropical oceans, and along coastal regions. It also enters lagoons on tropical island It is mostly observed on the surface. Divers and snorkelers can swim easily and safely with this curiously gentle shark.

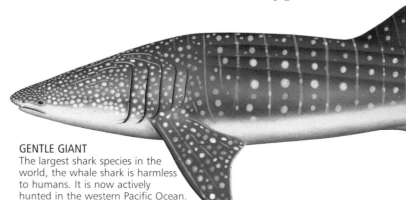

GENTLE GIANT
The largest shark species in the world, the whale shark is harmless to humans. It is now actively hunted in the western Pacific Ocean.

FEEDING AND BREEDING

The whale shark swims slowly near the surface, consuming small crustacean plankton, small fishes, such as sardines and anchovies, and even larger fishes such as mackerel. It has well-developed internal spongy filters at the gill arches, which help to retain small prey within its huge mouth. This mechanism may impede the flow of water through the mouth during swimming, which limits the amount of plankton the shark can strain. So, as well as filter feeding, it can also pump water into its mouth to feed on concentrated patches of plankton.

It is a prolific livebearer—some 300 embryos were found inside the female.

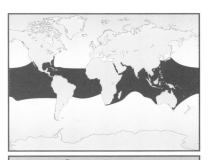

SNAPSHOT

OTHER NAMES **None**
SIZE AT BIRTH **18 inches (45 cm)**
DIET **Filter-feeds on plankton and small fishes**
HABITAT **Ocean and coastal zones, often entering lagoons**
DISTRIBUTION **Worldwide in tropics**

SIZE COMPARISON
■ Male 29½ feet (9 m)
□ Female 26¼ feet (8 m)

Zebra Shark

Stegostoma fasciatum

Maximum length: 11½ feet (3.5 m)

■ MAIN FEATURES

The zebra shark is found over tropical coral reefs. Its very long, broad tail and its coloring make it quite distinctive. The juvenile shark has zebra-like stripes (yellow on black), which give the shark its common name. It takes on a yellowish brown color with dark brown spotting as it reaches adulthood. Because of this adult coloration, it is also known as the leopard shark. This is the cause of some confusion, since there is another shark known as a leopard shark—a very different kind of cold-water species from the houndshark family, which occurs mainly in the eastern Pacific.

The zebra shark has small barbels on its snout, a small mouth, and small eyes. Its teeth are pointed, with each tooth having two smaller, lateral, flanking points. Prominent ridges run along its flanks.

This is a sluggish species. Divers sometimes find one resting

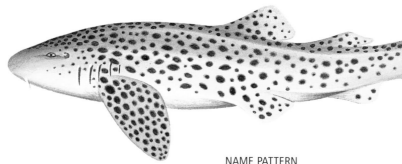

NAME PATTERN
The zebra shark is so named because the juveniles are black with yellow stripes, resembling the pattern on a zebra.

n the bottom during the day,
ropped up on its pectoral fins
ith its open mouth facing into
e current in order to obtain
xygen more easily from the water.

FEEDING AND BREEDING
he slender, flexible body of the
ebra shark allows it to wriggle
to narrow crevices in the reef,
earching for the shellfish,
ustaceans, and small, slow fishes
pon which it prefers to feed.

The shark is oviparous. It lays
rge, dark brown or purplish
ack egg cases, 5–7 inches
3–18 cm) in length. Fibers help
tach them to the seabed.

SNAPSHOT

OTHER NAMES **Leopard shark,
blind shark**
SIZE AT BIRTH **8 inches (20 cm)**
DIET **Mollusks, crustaceans, and
bony fishes**
HABITAT **Shallow water; common
in coral reefs**
DISTRIBUTION **Tropical western
Pacific to eastern Africa**

SIZE COMPARISON
Male and female 6½ feet (2 m)

Lamniformes

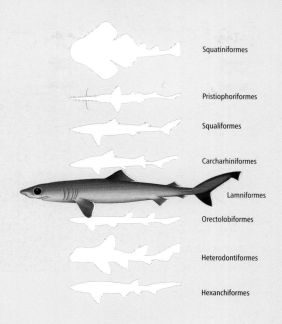

Squatiniformes

Pristiophoriformes

Squaliformes

Carcharhiniformes

Lamniformes

Orectolobiformes

Heterodontiformes

Hexanchiformes

LAMNIFORMES, WITH SEVEN families and some
15 species, are found in all seas except for high
Arctic and Antarctic latitudes. Most of them
have elongated snouts, long mouths that
reach behind the eyes, an anal fin, and
two spineless dorsal fins.

Basking Shark

Cetorhinus maximus

Maximum length: 49¼ feet (15 m);
few over 33 feet (10 m)

■ MAIN FEATURES
The basking shark is the second
largest fish in the world; the
largest is the whale shark. Its
huge size makes it easy to
identify, as do its very broad
gill slits that extend around
the top and bottom of the head.
The grayish brown body is
streamlined and stout, with a
strong, crescent-shaped tail fin
and lateral keels. The short snout
is narrow and conical, with huge

jaws that expand laterally when
the shark feeds.

Basking sharks are highly
migratory, appearing seasonally
specific locations and supportin
regional commercial fisheries—
they are taken for their flesh and
large liver.

■ FEEDING AND BREEDING
Basking sharks are frequent
visitors to both cold and warm
temperate waters, where they ta
advantage of plankton blooms i
coastal regions. They often enter
large bays to feed. You may see
them close to shore, swimming
slowly near the surface with

A MIGHTY FISH
This is the second largest species
of shark, and is occasionally
killed for its oil (squalene), fins,
skin, and meat.

outh wide open to form a very
ide "net" for capturing the
ankton. Water passes into the
outh and across the specialized
ll rakers, which strain out the
ankton before the water
erges through the gill slits.
is feeding posture is in distinct
ntrast to the long but narrow
outh opening of the feeding
hale shark.

Populations of basking sharks
e often segregated by sex and
ze. Very little is known about
eir reproduction, but it has
en noted that females reach
aturity at about 13–16½ feet
–5 m) long, and are thought to
ar live young.

SNAPSHOT

OTHER NAMES **Bone shark,
elephant shark, sailfish shark**
SIZE AT BIRTH **5–6½ feet
(1.5–2 m)**
DIET **Filter-feeds on plankton and
small crustaceans**
HABITAT **Coastal, usually seen
near the surface**
DISTRIBUTION **Most temperate
seas**

SIZE COMPARISON
■ Male 29¼ feet (8.9 m)
☐ Female 21⅓ feet (6.5 m)

Crocodile Shark

Pseudocarcharias kamoharai

Maximum length: 3¼ feet (1 m)

■ MAIN FEATURES
The crocodile shark, which is
the only species of the family
Pseudocarchariidae, is related to
the sand tiger shark. Its muscular
and highly streamlined body
looks like a mini-torpedo. The
first dorsal fin is about midway
between the small pectoral and
pelvic fins. The second dorsal fin
is much smaller.

The body is dark brown above,
grading to lighter underneath,
with dark blotches often scattered
over the sides and the bottom
surfaces. The head is long, the
snout conical, and the eyes larg[e]
The liver of this species contain[s]
squalene, which is a fine, low-
density oil that increases the
shark's buoyancy.

The shark is widespread
throughout the open oceans of t[he]
world, from the surface to depth[s]
of about 1,900 feet (590 m). It is
also sometimes seen offshore.

■ FEEDING AND BREEDING
The crocodile shark is thought t[o]
be a fast-swimming predator tha[t]
chases small prey, either near th[e]
surface at night or at depths of
1,000 feet (300 m) during the da[y]
The shark has powerful jaws an[d]

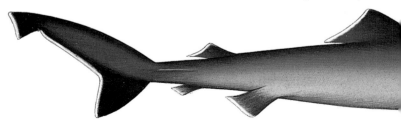

ELUSIVE STYLE
Little is known about the
crocodile shark. It is thought
to be nocturnal.

ng, thin, needlelike teeth,
nich are similar in shape to
ose found in the larger mako
arks. This combination of jaws
d teeth is designed for the
ocodile shark to grasp its small
d-water prey, including
rimp, lanternfishes, and squid.

Because it is essentially a
ep-water shark, little is known
out the crocodile shark's
productive biology, though
ere seem to be four young in
ch litter (two from each uterus).
ter exhausting their own yolk
pply, the developing embryos
parently eat all but one sibling
each uterus. They continue to
velop by feeding on eggs
oduced by the mother. It is
known how or why two
abryos coexist in this manner.

SNAPSHOT

OTHER NAMES **None**
SIZE AT BIRTH **16 inches (40 cm)**
DIET **Probably small fishes, squid, and crustaceans**
HABITAT **Oceanic, probably mid-water, from the surface to 1,900 feet (590 m), and occasionally inshore**
DISTRIBUTION **All tropical and subtropical seas**

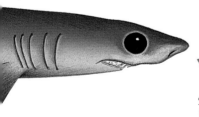

SIZE COMPARISON
■ Male 3¼ feet (95 cm)
☐ Female 3 feet (90 cm)

Goblin Shark

Mitsukurina owstoni

Maximum length: 12¾ feet (3.9 m)

■ MAIN FEATURES

Perhaps the most mysterious and bizarre of all sharks, the goblin shark is the only species of its family. Its light pink body is long but thin. The flesh has a soft, watery texture, which probably helps it to maintain neutral buoyancy, important in what is thought to be a slow-swimming species. The two dorsal fins are similar in size, while the anal fin is well developed. The tail consists almost entirely of a single, long upper lobe.

Very little is known about the biology and ecology of this shark. It occurs near the bottom on continental and island shelves and slopes. Living in such deep waters, it is rarely seen or collected. However, it is found occasionally in shallow water near the shore.

■ FEEDING

The goblin shark has a long snout flattened in the shape of a paddle. The nostrils are located immediately in front of the mouth. The teeth at the fron

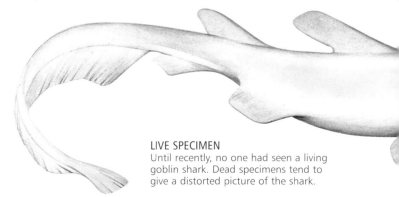

LIVE SPECIMEN
Until recently, no one had seen a living goblin shark. Dead specimens tend to give a distorted picture of the shark.

its narrow, pointed jaw are ng and needlelike, ideal for asping small fish. The teeth at e back of the mouth are small d form a crushing or grinding ate for processing captured ey. The goblin shark probably ostly feeds on small fishes, ustaceans, and squid, and its ddle-like snout is thought to d its electrosensory system in tecting and capturing a meal. In addition, its jaw is highly ecialized to project rapidly om the head. This makes the blin shark a very efficient edator, capable of quickly asping or sucking prey into mouth in a single bite.

SNAPSHOT

OTHER NAMES **Elfin shark**
SIZE AT BIRTH **Unknown**
DIET **Fragile, pointed teeth indicate soft-bodied prey such as pelagic squid**
HABITAT **Upper continental slope, near the bottom at 1,180–1,800 feet (360–550 m)**
DISTRIBUTION **Scattered tropical and temperate locations**

SIZE COMPARISON
Male and female 9½ feet (2.9 m)

Great White Shark

Carcharodon carcharias

Maximum length: 24 feet (7.3 m)

■ MAIN FEATURES
The white shark is the largest of the flesh-eating sharks, and it has featured heavily in film and literature. Great white sharks are responsible for the majority of unprovoked attacks on people in cool waters and they can kill humans. However, the number of attacks is usually fewer than ten a year. By diving inside a steel cage, it is possible to see them in relative safety.

Little is known of the shark's biology and behavior, though information can be deduced from its physical attributes.

The great white shark is a robust, torpedo-shaped, conical-snouted species. Unlike most sharks, but like other mackerel sharks, the upper and lower lobe of its tail are almost equal in size

This indicates that the shark swims constantly and that it may sometimes swim rapidly. It differs from its relatives in that it has nearly symmetrical triangular teeth with serrated edges, and it is huge.

DANGEROUS TYPE
The largest of the flesh-eating sharks, the great white is considered to be the most dangerous temperate shark to humans. As fishing is seriously depleting numbers, the species is now protected.

FEEDING AND BREEDING

The great white generally prefers shallow, cool, coastal waters, but is occasionally seen as close to the equator as Hawaii, USA. During the day, the adult sharks search for the seals and sea lions that are an important part of their diet.

Females give birth to seven to nine live pups per litter, and are thought to produce only four to six litters in a lifetime. The young do not mature until they are about 10 to 12 years old, so the species is extremely vulnerable to overfishing.

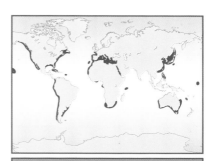

SNAPSHOT

OTHER NAMES White shark, white death, white pointer, blue pointer
SIZE AT BIRTH 3–4 feet (90–120 cm)
DIET Seals, sea lions, dolphins, turtles, other sharks, seabirds
HABITAT Coastal cooler waters, surface to 4,200 feet (1,280 m)
DISTRIBUTION Worldwide in temperate seas

SIZE COMPARISON
Male and female 11⅕ feet (3.4 m)

Megamouth Shark

Megachasma pelagios

Maximum length: 17 feet (5.2 m)

■ MAIN FEATURES
The accidental capture of a large, black, blubbery shark off Hawaii, USA, in 1976 was the shark discovery of last century. The creature had become entangled in a deep-water net line. It had a large head, a huge distending mouth about 3⅓ feet (1 m) wide, and over 100 rows of small teeth. Other characteristics indicated a relationship with the ecologically disparate white shark and the makos. A new genus, species, and family of vertebrates were created—the megamouth shark. Its scientific name comes from the Greek to mean "giant yawner of the open sea." Only nine more megamouth sharks have been found. They range in color from dark brown to gray to black. Not surprisingly, however, we know very little about its biology.

■ FEEDING AND BREEDING
It lives in the open ocean, often a great depths, which may explain the rarity of encounters. It appears to be a plankton feeder,

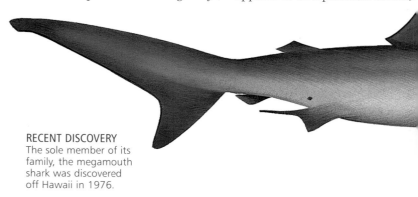

RECENT DISCOVERY
The sole member of its family, the megamouth shark was discovered off Hawaii in 1976.

...ke the whale shark and the ...asking shark. It swims slowly ...rough the open ocean, filtering ...nall shrimps and other prey ...om the water as it goes.

The megamouth shark appears ...spend the day feeding in deep ...ater, and comes up to shallower ...ater at night. The silvery lining ...its mouth cavity is luminous, ...d most probably reflective so ...at when shrimps and other ...ustaceans with bioluminescence ...ter the open, cavernous mouth, ...ey create a tiny beam of light ...at may attract other such prey.

Nothing is known of the ...productive biology or litter ...mbers of this species.

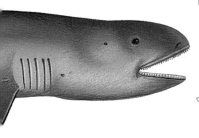

SIZE COMPARISON
Male and female 17 feet (5.2 m)

Porbeagle Shark

Lamna nasus

Maximum length: 10 feet (3 m)

■ MAIN FEATURES
The porbeagle and its North Pacific relative, the salmon shark, are the smallest of the five mackerel sharks. They are still an impressive sight at 350–500 pounds (158–225 kg).

The porbeagle's stout body is dark blue-gray to brown dorsally, and white underneath. It has a patch of white on the trailing edge of the first dorsal fin. The porbeagle and salmon shark are the only sharks with a secondary keel at the base of their crescent-shaped tails. This assists the efficiency of its side-to-side swimming movement, cutting the water around it.

The mackerel sharks are unique among sharks for their heat-exchanging circulatory system, which makes them, functionally, warm-blooded. They can capture the heat generated by their swimming muscles and, through a complex arrangement of microscopic arteries and veins, use it to heat the blood. This blood is directed throughout the body, to the muscles, internal organs, and brain. As a result, their body temperature is higher than that of the surrounding water.

CLEVER COMBUSTION
An internal heating system provides these sharks with increased muscle strength and allows more rapid nervous-system activity in frigid habitats.

FEEDING AND BREEDING

The fast-swimming porbeagle shark inhabits the continental shelves in cold waters, down to depths of 1,200 feet (370 m). With its sharp, slender teeth, it feeds on mackerel and squid when it ventures into open waters, and also on cod, hake, flounder, and other bottom-dwelling fish. Like all mackerel sharks, but unlike most sharks that live on the bottom, the porbeagle shark must swim continuously in order to breathe. It reproduces viviparously, without a placental connection. As with some other mackerel sharks, the older embryos feed on some of the eggs and smaller embryos in the uterus.

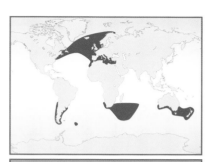

SNAPSHOT

OTHER NAMES Mackerel shark
SIZE AT BIRTH 2½ feet (75 cm)
DIET Bony fishes, other sharks, and squid
HABITAT Inshore and oceanic from the surface to 1,200 feet (370 m)
DISTRIBUTION Most temperate seas except North Pacific

SIZE COMPARISON
■ Male 8¼ feet (2.5 m)
☐ Female 7 feet (2.1 m)

Sand Tiger Shark

Carcharias taurus

Maximum length: 10½ feet (3.2 m)

■ MAIN FEATURES

Depending on where you are in the world, the sand tiger shark may be known as the spotted raggedtooth or gray nurse shark. It is one of four species belonging to the sand tiger family, a group of large, fearsome-looking sharks that swim slowly with their mouths open, exposing long, narrow, needlelike teeth. Their bodies are stout, with two large dorsal fins. The elongated tails have a long upper lobe; there is a precaudal pit but no caudal keels.

The shark has a short, flattene snout. Its dorsal fins are about equal in size, with the first dorsa fin located closer to the pelvic fins than to the pectoral fins. It is bronzy above, then gradually becomes paler below. Juveniles have reddish or brownish spots scattered on the tail and rear of the body, which tend to fade wit age. There are three rows of large teeth on each side of the midline of the upper jaw.

The sand tiger shark is found in shallow bays, sandy coastal waters, and rocky or tropical ree from shallow waters down to about 655 feet (200 m). Divers frequently find large numbers in aggregations around rocky outcroppings in offshore waters.

FLOATING MECHANISM
The sand tiger shark is able to hover motionless in the water by swallowing surface air and holding it in its stomach, thus achieving near-neutral buoyancy.

ssentially gentle sharks, they
sually become aggressive only
 they are provoked.

FEEDING AND BREEDING
heir diet consists of large and
mall bony fishes, small sharks,
ays, crustaceans, and squid.
The shark is known to make
airly long coastal migrations,
most probably for reproductive
urposes. It is oviphagous. In
ach of the two uterine chambers,
he first embryo to hatch, at about
½ inches (17 cm), kills and
evours the other developing
iblings. The two embryos
ontinue to feed on the other eggs
nside the separate uterine
hambers. After a gestation period
f eight to nine months, the two
ve young are born.

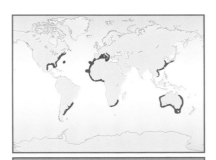

SNAPSHOT

OTHER NAMES Raggedtooth shark,
gray nurse shark, spotted
raggedtooth shark, sand shark
SIZE AT BIRTH 3¼ feet (1 m)
DIET Fishes, sharks, rays, crabs
HABITAT Coastal, from sandy
beaches to 655 feet (200 m)
DISTRIBUTION Widespread

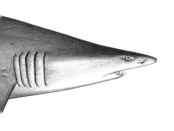

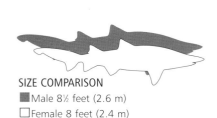

SIZE COMPARISON
◼ Male 8½ feet (2.6 m)
☐ Female 8 feet (2.4 m)

Shortfin Mako

Isurus oxyrinchus

Maximum length: 13 feet (4 m)

■ MAIN FEATURES

The shortfin mako shark is the most spindle-shaped shark of the mackerel family, with a long, conical snout, short pectoral fins, and a crescent-shaped caudal fin. Its back is indigo blue, and the belly is white. Its teeth, visible even when its mouth is closed, are long, slender, smooth-edged daggers. The less common longfin mako *Isurus paucus* has longer pectoral fins and a blunter snout.

The shortfin mako, the shark featured in Ernest Hemingway's novel *The Old Man and the Sea*, is known as a sport fish, capable of spectacular leaps 20 feet (6 m) in the air when hooked, and of achieving bursts of speed of more than 22 miles (35 km) per hour.

Shortfin makos live offshore in tropical and temperate waters, from the surface down to 500 feet (150 m). Rarely encountered, they may occasionally be seen by open water divers. They are dangerous and have attacked humans.

SPORTING TYPE
The active shortfin mako is sought by anglers not only for its tasty flesh, but also for its fighting and jumping abilities. Although potentially dangerous, it is rarely encountered by humans.

st attacks, however, have
curred on fishing boats, when
angry mako has been captured.

FEEDING AND BREEDING

ortfin makos use their speed to
pture oceanic fish and squid.
rge makos also catch billfish
d whales. They have been
cked traveling 1,322 miles
128 km) in 37 days, an average
36 miles (58 km) a day.
Shortfin makos are viviparous,
lack a placental connection.
ters of 4 to 16 pups are not
common. Older embryos eat
me of the eggs and smaller
bryos while still in the uterus.

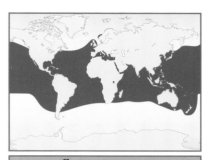

SNAPSHOT

OTHER NAMES Blue pointer,
mackerel shark, snapper shark,
mako shark, bonito shark
SIZE AT BIRTH 2–2½ feet (60–70 cm)
DIET Bony fishes, sharks, squid,
oceanic whales and dolphins
HABITAT Coastal and oceanic, from
surface to 500 feet (150 m)
DISTRIBUTION All warm seas

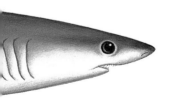

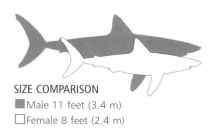

SIZE COMPARISON
■ Male 11 feet (3.4 m)
☐ Female 8 feet (2.4 m)

Thresher Shark

Alopias vulpinus

Maximum length: 18 feet (5.5 m)

■ MAIN FEATURES

The common thresher is one of three thresher sharks. These large, pelagic sharks are immediately recognizable by their long tails. They have a short, conical snout, large eyes placed well forward on the head, and a husky, spindle-shaped body. The first dorsal fin is much larger than the second. The broad pectoral fins provide lift when swimming—these sharks have enough power to leap out of the water.

The jaws are relatively small, with remarkably efficient tiny, sharp teeth used for capturing cephalopods and schooling fishes. To frighten prey into tight groups for easier capture, these sharks slap the water surface with their long tail.

Common threshers can be distinguished from their relatives by the position of the first dorsal fin, with its leading edge above the trailing edge of the pectoral fins. The pectoral fins are curved.

The body of the shark is dark blue-gray above, with a sharp, ragged break marking the edge of its white underside. There are prominent labial furrows at the sides of the jaws.

LOCATION

The common thresher shark is widespread in tropical and temperate waters. It is commonly seen swimming at the surface in coastal waters, but also occurs at depths of 1,200 feet (365 m). It is best viewed from boats or by snorkelers in open water. While not aggressive toward humans, this is a large shark. Its power, and its tail, should be respected.

The thresher is targeted by fisheries worldwide for its fins and meat. Consequently, populations are diminishing, particularly in coastal areas.

STUNNING BODY

The thresher shark uses its elongate tail to herd prey into groups and stun them.

SIZE COMPARISON
■ Male 15 feet (4.6 m)
☐ Female 11¾ feet (3.6 m)

Carcharhiniformes

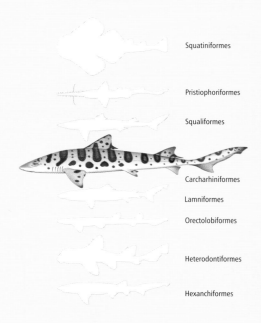

Squatiniformes

Pristiophoriformes

Squaliformes

Carcharhiniformes

Lamniformes

Orectolobiformes

Heterodontiformes

Hexanchiformes

THE ORDER CARCHARHINIFORMES dominates the world's
shark fauna, with approximately 197 known species.
The group is varied in a gradient from the most primitive
small, inactive, small-toothed catsharks, through the
intermediate houndsharks and weasel sharks, to the
powerful requiem sharks and hammerheads
that dominate the warm seas.

Atlantic Weasel Shark

Paragaleus pectoralis

Maximum length: 4¹/₂ feet (1.4 m)

■ MAIN FEATURES

The Atlantic weasel shark has a small to medium-sized, slender body, very similar to that of the requiem shark. There are seven species of weasel shark (family Hemigaleidae) described to date.

Its snout is moderately long. The eyes are large and nearly circular, and they have nictitating membranes. The teeth are small, and set in a short, small mouth.

This reflects the fact that the weasel shark specializes in feeding upon soft-bodied cephalopods (squid and octopu[s]). The spiracles are tiny, and its nostrils are without barbels.

The weasel shark has two dorsal fins; the first is clearly larger than the second and is positioned in front of the pelvic fins. The shark's pectoral fins ar[e] long and pointed, and its anal fin is considerably smaller than the second dorsal. There are precaudal pits and the asymmet[?] rical caudal fin has a strong ventral lobe.

The coloring is blue gray to bronze with yellow stripes and a white underside.

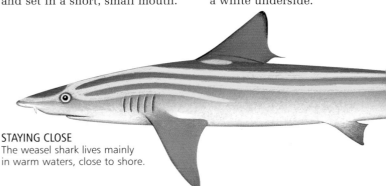

STAYING CLOSE
The weasel shark lives mainly
in warm waters, close to shore.

This species is rarely sighted d therefore poorly under- od, so little is known of its roductive habits. However, weasel sharks are known be viviparous, giving birth one to four pups per litter.

LOCATION
e Atlantic weasel shark is an hore shark, occurring in shelf ters at modest depths, from intertidal to about 330 feet 0 m). It is the only species in family to inhabit the eastern antic. The six other weasel rk species are characteristic he Indo-West Pacific, from th Africa and the Red Sea apan and Australia.

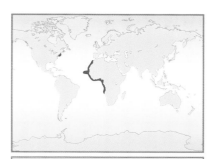

SNAPSHOT

OTHER NAMES **None**
SIZE AT BIRTH **16 inches (40 cm)**
DIET **Primarily squid and octopus; also small fishes**
HABITAT **Shallow water to 330 feet (100 m)**
DISTRIBUTION **Tropical western Africa**

SIZE COMPARISON
Male and female 3¼ feet (1 m)

Barbeled Houndshark

Leptocharias smithii

Maximum length: 2³/₄ feet (83 cm)

■ MAIN FEATURES

The barbeled houndshark is the only member of the unusual family Leptochariidae. While closely related to the requiem sharks and houndsharks, many of its characteristics are unique. It is a small species, with an elongated gray or brownish body. The first of two dorsal fins is between the pectoral and pelvic fins, while the second is positioned above the anal fin.

The head is small and the ey are large and catlike. The nasal flaps are modified into short, slender barbels. The corners of the mouth have long labial furrows, and the teeth of both jaws are small, with narrow cus and cusplets.

The barbeled houndshark is usually found in coastal areas, both inshore in waters about 33 feet (10 m) deep, and also above the adjacent shelf at dept of about 250 feet (75 m). It can approached, with caution, by experienced divers.

This shark is commercially fished by local fisheries for its meat and skin.

PIGGY SHARK
The barbeled houndshark is a scavenger. All sorts of unlikely objects, including feathers and flowers, have been found in its stomach.

FEEDING AND BREEDING

The barbeled houndshark prefers muddy bottom areas, especially near river mouths, where it feeds on crustaceans, small fishes, and cephalopods. Males have larger teeth than females, possibly for grasping the females during copulation. The species is essentially an omnivorous scavenger and all sorts of indigestible objects, including feathers and flowers, have been found in its stomach.

Females mature when about 20 inches (50 cm) long. They have a gestation period of at least four months and give birth to litters of about seven live young, probably in October.

SNAPSHOT

OTHER NAMES **None**
SIZE AT BIRTH **12 inches (30 cm)**
DIET **Bottom-living crustaceans, small fishes, and fish eggs**
HABITAT **Bottom dweller at depths of 33–250 feet (10–75 m)**
DISTRIBUTION **West Africa from Mauritania to Angola**

SIZE COMPARISON
■ Male 2⅓ feet (70 cm)
☐ Female 2¼ feet (67 cm)

Blacktip Reef Shark

Carcharhinus melanopterus

Maximum length: 6 feet (1.8 m)

■ MAIN FEATURES
Blacktip reef sharks are requiem
sharks (family Carcharhinidae)
and are easily recognized by the
very distinct black marks on their
fins, particularly the first dorsal
and caudal fins. They also have
a conspicuous white slash along
their flanks. They are different
from blacktip sharks—larger
sharks with thin, black tips on
most fins that live mainly in the
open ocean. Blacktip reef sharks
are small to medium in size, with
a short, blunt snout. Their teeth
are narrow, sharp, and strongly
serrated, designed for eating the
reef fish that are their main food.

They are viviparous, with
the yolk sac being attached by a
placenta. Litters number from two
to four. The pups are born after
a gestation of about 16 months,
and are 13–20 inches (33–50 cm)
long at birth.

■ LOCATION
Blacktip reef sharks are the most
common sharks in the shallow

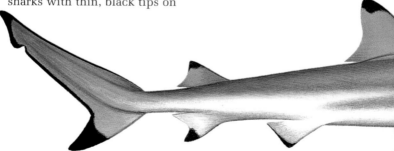

PUBLIC TYPES
Because they are a small, hardy species, blacktip
reef sharks populate public aquariums worldwide.

lagoons and coral reefs of the tropical Pacific and Indian Oceans, along with whitetip reef sharks and gray reef sharks.

Divers and snorkelers commonly see them patrolling in shallow waters from about 12 inches (30 cm) deep. Divers will find them in reef passes, while waders and snorkelers will see them in lagoons, their dorsal and caudal fins above the surface. They will attack speared fish, and are curious, but not aggressive, around divers. On rare occasions, however, they have bitten waders on the legs and ankles, probably attracted by the splashing.

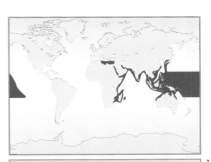

SNAPSHOT

OTHER NAMES **Blacktip shark, guliman**
SIZE AT BIRTH **13–20 inches (33–50 cm)**
DIET **Primarily reef fishes, but also crustaceans and cephalopods**
HABITAT **Shallow reef flats to outer reef edge**
DISTRIBUTION **Tropical central Pacific to eastern Africa**

SIZE COMPARISON
■ Male 4½ feet (1.4 m)
□ Female 3⅔ feet (1.1 m)

Blue Shark

Prionace glauca

Maximum length: 12½ feet (3.9 m)

■ MAIN FEATURES

The blue shark, one of the most attractive sharks, is large and slender. Its upper body is indigo blue, the sides are bright blue, and the belly is markedly white. With its long, narrow, pointed pectoral fins, long snout, and large eyes, it is unmistakable.

This requiem shark is found in the open ocean throughout the tropics and into cooler seas. In the tropics, it often enters deeper, cooler water, while in temperate coastal waters it comes close to the edge of kelp beds, where divers may see it. It migrates regularly in the Atlantic, following the Gulf Stream to Europe, moving south along the African coast, then returning to the Caribbean.

Open-water divers may see these sharks, particularly if the sharks have been attracted by chum. Dive operators offer tours using cages off southern California, USA, and elsewhere. Although attacks are unlikely, excited sharks have occasionally taken a nip at an unwary diver.

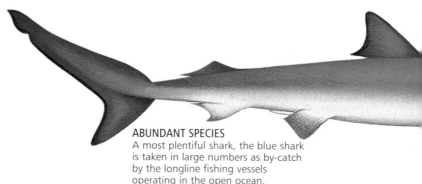

ABUNDANT SPECIES
A most plentiful shark, the blue shark is taken in large numbers as by-catch by the longline fishing vessels operating in the open ocean.

FEEDING AND BREEDING

Blue sharks feed ravenously on large schools of squid, but are also very opportunistic and will decimate a floating whale or porpoise carcass. Fisheries consider them a menace because they attack nets and eat fish caught on lines.

Although not yet observed, blue shark courtship is thought to be very lively. Males bite the females' shoulders; fortunately, females' skin is three times as thick as that of the males.

Females reach maturity at about five years of age. They mate and can store sperm in the oviducal gland for nearly 12 months, after which fertilization occurs. Litters range from 4 to 135 pups, depending on the size of the mother.

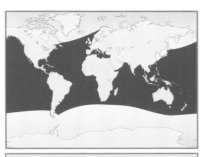

SNAPSHOT

OTHER NAMES **Blue whaler, great blue shark, blue dog**
SIZE AT BIRTH **16 inches (40 cm)**
DIET **Pelagic fishes, squid**
HABITAT **Oceanic, from the surface to 1,150 feet (350 m), and close to shore in some locations**
DISTRIBUTION **All warm seas**

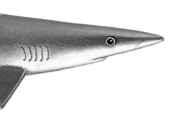

SIZE COMPARISON
■ Male 9¼ feet (2.8 m)
☐ Female 8¼ feet (2.5 m)

Brown Catshark

Apristurus brunneus

Maximum length: 2¼ feet (68 cm)

■ MAIN FEATURES
With more than 100 species, the catshark family Scyliorhinidae is the largest of the shark families. The name comes from the catlike shape and color of the eyes. Typical of the family is the brown catshark. It has a long, slender body, with two dorsal fins of similar size, small pectoral fins, and a long anal fin that reaches to the start of the elongate caudal fin. This harmless species has small eyes with nictitating membranes, small teeth, relatively large gill slits, and a long, broad snout. Their coloring is chocolate brown on the upper body and underside, with pale fin margins.

The brown catshark is oviparous, laying one egg at a time in a case that is 2 inches (5 cm) long. It is believed that the pup hatches after a period of about 12 months.

Although quite a common deep-water shark, little is known about the brown catshark or any of the other species in the genus Apristurus. Attempts have been made to keep the species in captivity, but with no success.

■ OTHER FAMILY MEMBERS
More striking than the brown catshark is the coral catshark *Atelomycterus marmoratus* (species Marmoratus). It is a rather small species with a dramatic body coloration of whit

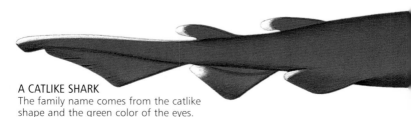

A CATLIKE SHARK
The family name comes from the catlike shape and the green color of the eyes.

spots on a dark background ‌ading to a white underbelly. ‌he dorsal fins, which are almost ‌ual in size, have white spots on ‌eir tips. The tail fin is short.

Unique features include the ‌hort caudal fin, the long labial ‌rrows at the corners of the ‌outh, and nasal flaps that ‌xtend to the front of the mouth. ‌he eyes are set in front of large ‌iracles, which are used to move ‌ater into the gill chambers when ‌e shark is at rest or feeding.

The Australian marbled ‌atshark *Atelomycterus macleayi*, ‌hich occurs in northern ‌ustralia, is similar in appear-‌ce to the coral catshark, but ‌n be distinguished by the gray ‌ddle-like markings along its ‌ack, and small, black spots over ‌ost of its body.

SIZE COMPARISON
■ Male 21 inches (53 cm)
☐ Female 18 inches (45 cm)

Bull Shark

Carcharhinus leucas

Maximum length: 11½ feet (3.5 m)

■ MAIN FEATURES
This requiem shark has a unique appearance. It has a very blunt, rounded snout, small eyes, a pointed first dorsal fin, and dusky fin tips. It will eat almost anything it can capture, including other sharks, rays, fishes, turtles, birds, dolphins, mollusks, crustaceans, and things that fall overboard, such as cattle, dogs, and even people.

It is viviparous, and selects estuaries as pupping grounds for litters of between 1 and 13 pups, which are born after a gestation of almost 12 months.

■ LOCATION
This large, stout, and sluggish gray shark is widespread along continental coasts. It also enters rivers and lakes, and is therefore known by such names as the Lake Nicaragua shark and the Zambezi shark. It was also thought to be the rare Ganges shark, but this is now known to be a separate, distinct species.

In the Americas, it is found close to shore in estuaries and shallow marine habitats from just a few feet deep to 100 feet (30 m). The bull shark can tolerate highly salty sea water and fresh water—it has been recorded as far as

VULNERABLE TYPES
Because they live close to shore and in rivers and lakes, bull sharks are vulnerable to fisheries.

750 miles (2,800 km) up the Mississippi River in the USA and 2,500 miles (4,000 km) up the Amazon River in Peru.

The bull shark's wide distribution range provides it with ample opportunity to encounter, attack, and consume people, and because it has been confused with other similar-looking requiem sharks, it seems likely that it is responsible for even more attacks than those with which it is credited. This makes it more dangerous than the great white or tiger sharks. The famous Matawan Creek incident of 1916, when sharks killed four people and injured one along the New Jersey shore over a 12-day period, was probably the work of bull sharks.

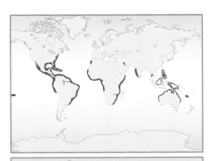

SNAPSHOT

OTHER NAMES Lake Nicaragua and Zambezi shark, freshwater whaler

SIZE AT BIRTH 22–32 inches (55–80 cm)

DIET Omnivorous, eating turtles, birds, dolphins, and crustaceans, but preferring bony fishes

HABITAT Estuaries, rivers, and coastal waters to 100 feet (30 m)

DISTRIBUTION All tropical and subtropical seas

SIZE COMPARISON
■ Male 8 feet (2.4 m)
□ Female 7½ feet (2.3 m)

Dusky Smoothhound

Mustelus canis

Maximum length: 5 feet (1.5 m)

■ MAIN FEATURES
The dusky smoothhound of the western Atlantic is one of the 20 or so species of the genus Mustelus (family Triakidae).

It is a relatively small shark with a slender body, two large dorsal fins (the first being considerably larger than the second), an anal fin which is about half the size of the second dorsal fin, a long caudal fin, and broad, pointed pectoral fins. Its snout is long and pointe it has oval eyes with nictitating membranes, and it has small spiracles.

The coloring of the dusky smoothhound is uniformly grayish brown with a white underside, though it is able to alter its color to blend in with it environment. This enables it to camouflage itself from predators, and to surprise prey.

■ LOCATION
The species mainly occurs on the continental shelves and slopes from near the surface to depths c

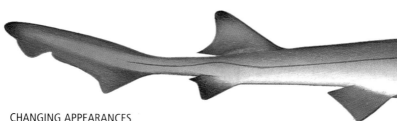

CHANGING APPEARANCES
The dusky smoothhound shark is able to camouflage itself from predators by altering its color to blend in with its environment.

me 650 feet (200 m). Dusky moothhounds are abundant, d divers will often see them ing on the seabed in shallow astal waters. They occasionally so enter fresh water. Since they e not at all aggressive, they can approached with safety.

As for many other sharks, ater temperature plays an portant role in controlling the igration routes of the dusky moothhound shark. It is found waters where the temperature about 66°F (19°C). As the water mperature changes with the asons, the dusky shark moves ound to follow the water of its referred temperature.

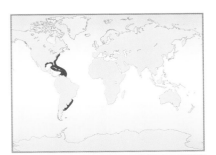

SNAPSHOT

OTHER NAMES **None**
SIZE AT BIRTH **13–15 inches (33–38 cm)**
DIET **Primarily large crabs and lobsters, also shellfish, squid, and small bony fishes**
HABITAT **Continental shelves and slopes from near surface to 650 feet (200 m)**
DISTRIBUTION **Western Atlantic from Massachusetts to Venezuela, Brazil to Argentina, and the Gulf of Mexico**

SIZE COMPARISON
Male and female 3½ feet (105 cm)

False Catshark

Pseudotriakis microdon

Maximum length: 10 feet (3 m)

■ MAIN FEATURES
Sharks are members of marine bottom communities from the sunlit shallows of intertidal pools to the dark, abyssal plains thousands of feet deep. While many of the species that live on or near the bottom belong to families that are familiar and well known to researchers, there are also species from smaller families about which little is understood. Among these species are the finback catsharks, barbeled houndsharks, weasel sharks, and the false catsharks.

The false catshark is a deep-water shark that lives on shelf slopes from 660–5,000 feet (200–1,500 m). It is thought to be the only species of the family Pseudotriakidae, which is closely related to the catshark family.

It is long and slender, and its distinguishing feature is the long base and low height of the keel-like first dorsal fin. The eye is oval and catlike, with the nictitating membrane reduced in size. There is a large spiracle. The jaw of the false catshark is large, and the back rows of its many

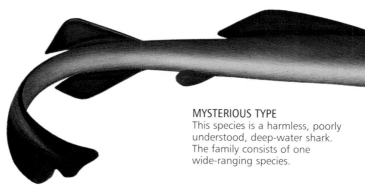

MYSTERIOUS TYPE
This species is a harmless, poorly understood, deep-water shark. The family consists of one wide-ranging species.

...ws of teeth are comblike. Its ...dy is watery and soft, which ...y help to give it the neutral ...oyancy that suits its somewhat ...dentary life on or near the ...ttom of the ocean.

FEEDING AND BREEDING
...e false catshark most probably ...ds on deep-water fishes and ...vertebrates. Females are ...ought to reach sexual maturity ...en about 7¼ feet (2.2 m) long, ...d bear two to four live young. ...ese sharks employ what is ...led intra-uterine oophagy, ...process whereby the embryos ...d on unfertilized eggs during ...e period of gestation.

SIZE COMPARISON
■ Male 8¼ feet (2.5 m)
☐ Female 7½ feet (2.3 m)

Galápagos Shark

Carcharhinus galapagensis

Maximum length: 12 feet (3.6 m)

■ MAIN FEATURES

The Galápagos shark is a large, grayish requiem shark without any distinctive markings. It looks similar to the gray reef shark and the silvertip shark, except that it lacks their conspicuous white or black coloration on its fins. Its most distinctive feature is a ridge between its dorsal fins.

The Galápagos shark is generally not a threat to divers, and prefers to avoid them, so there has never been a report of an attack on a diver. The same i not true, however, for swimmers Swimmers have been attacked and consumed by this shark. Lik the gray reef shark, the Galápago shark performs a seemingly awkward threat display before attacking a potential competitor or predator.

The shark was named in 190! after specimens found in the waters of the Galápagos Islands. It has since been found around most tropical oceanic islands,

THREAT DISPLAY
Like the gray reef shark, the Galápagos shark performs a threat display before attacking a potential competitor or pre

nging from inshore to well fshore. It prefers clear water, d can be seen beyond the deep ef edge, either near the surface in groups near the bottom.

FEEDING AND BREEDING
e Galápagos shark feeds on ttom-dwelling fish, as well as uid and octopus.

There are between 6 and 16 ung in a litter. They are born ive and remain in nursery areas, here the water is shallower than e area inhabited by the adults of e group. This adaptation is not common in a number of shark ecies to avoid cannibalism.

SNAPSHOT

OTHER NAMES **None**
SIZE AT BIRTH **23–32 inches (57–80 cm)**
DIET **Reef fishes**
HABITAT **Just beyond outer reef edge**
DISTRIBUTION **Cosmopolitan in tropics, generally near oceanic islands**

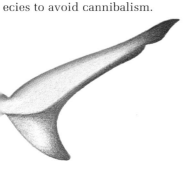

SIZE COMPARISON
■ Male 9 feet (2.7 m)
□ Female 7½ feet (2.3 m)

Graceful Catshark

Proscyllium habereri

Maximum length: 26 inches (65 cm)

■ Main features

The graceful catshark is one of the finback catsharks Proscylliidae, close relatives of the catshark family. Their first dorsal fin is above or in front of the pelvic fins, while in true catsharks, it is behind them. The two dorsal fins are of about equal size, with the second fin positioned above the anal fin. These small, bottom-dwelling sharks have slender, elongated bodies. The large, catlike eyes have a nictitating membrane, usually reduced in size, and there is a prominent spiracle behind the eye, which is used for ventilation. The labial furrows in the corner of the mouth are small or absent, the teeth in the back of the mouth are comblike, and there are no nasal barbels.

This species is distinguished by the pattern of dark spots that covers its fins and small body. The graceful catshark belongs to a small family of six species, living in the Caribbean or the western Pacific and Indian

RECLUSIVE TYPE
Like all finback sharks, the graceful catshark is a rarely seen and poorly understood species.

eans. It is found above island
d continental shelves in warm
mperate and tropical waters at
pths of between 165–330 feet
)–100 m).

FEEDING AND BREEDING
e diet of the graceful catshark
cludes small bony fishes, crabs,
d cephalopods.

Little is known about this
imal's reproductive biology,
that of other finback sharks.
s thought that the species is
iparous, but it is unknown how
any eggs the females produce
ch year.

SNAPSHOT

OTHER NAMES **None**
SIZE AT BIRTH **Unknown**
DIET **Bony fishes and crabs**
HABITAT **Continental shelves at
depths of 165–330 feet
(50–100 m)**
DISTRIBUTION **Western Indo-
Pacific, from Southern Japan
to Indonesia**

SIZE COMPARISON
■ Male 20 inches (50 cm)
□ Female 16½ inches (42 cm)

Great Hammerhead

Sphyrna mokarran

Maximum length: 20 feet (6 m)

■ MAIN FEATURES

The great hammerhead is easily identified by its thick, broad head, which has an almost flat leading edge, except for an indentation in the center. This requiem shark is a large, stout shark, gray-brown above, grading to a paler color below. The first dorsal fin is extremely high and pointed, with a curved rear margin. The base of the anal fin is much longer than that of the second dorsal fin.

This species is distributed in nearly all warm temperate and tropical waters. It occurs in coastal areas above continental and island shelves, and in adjacent offshore waters to dept of about 260 feet (80 m). Divers are likely to see it in shallow waters close to shore, especially near coral reef drop-offs and adjacent sand habitats. It makes long migrations to cooler waters during the summer months.

■ FEEDING AND BREEDING

The great hammerhead has a ver keen olfactory sense, and is an impressive predator. Its diet consists of many mobile fishes associated with the water colum including sardines, herring,

DANGEROUS EXCEPTION
Although most hammerhead species are harmless to humans, the great hammerhead is an exception and has attacked on occasion.

rpon, and jacks, and benthic
species such as grouper, sea cats,
catfish, and croaker. But this
shark is best known for its
preference for other elasmobranchs, such as stingrays, skates,
and other sharks. In its voracious
and unique predatory behavior
toward stingrays, the great
hammerhead uses the side of its
head to pin a fleeing ray to the
bottom. It then rotates its head to
the side and cleanly bites off a
large chunk of the ray's wing. It
continues to circle and feed on
the incapacitated prey until it has
been totally consumed.

Females reach sexual maturity
when about 10 feet (3 m) long.
They usually produce 20 to 40
young per litter.

SNAPSHOT

OTHER NAMES Scoop hammerhead
SIZE AT BIRTH 2⅕ feet (65 cm)
DIET Other sharks and rays
HABITAT Coastal and above
continental shelves, from surface
to 260 feet (80 m)
DISTRIBUTION All tropical seas;
not found in Hawaii

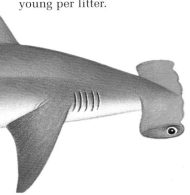

SIZE COMPARISON
■ Male 12 feet (3.7 m)
☐ Female 10 feet (3 m)

Gray Reef Shark

Carcharhinus amblyrhynchos

Maximum length: 8½ feet (2.6 m)

■ MAIN FEATURES
The gray reef shark, or longnose blacktail shark, is one of the most common requiem sharks on Indo-Pacific coral reefs, and is seen in the reef passes.

It is similar in shape and general appearance to the silvertip shark, although usually smaller. Some specimens have a narrow, white edging on the first dorsal fin, but they lack the bold, white-edged margins of the silvertip's tail and pectoral fins. The body of the gray reef shark is bronze to gray with a pale underside. One of the shark's most distinctive features is the black banding on the posterior margin of the caudal fin.

■ FEEDING AND BREEDING
The teeth are triangular with fine serrations. It feeds on small reef fish. An inquisitive animal, it is attracted to the low-frequency underwater sounds and commotion caused by speared fish—there have been many stories of gray reef sharks taking fish off the end of unsuspecting spearfishers' spears.

THREAT OF ATTACK
The gray reef shark precedes an attack with a complex threat display that includes head wagging, depressed pectoral fins, and an arched back.

Attacks against potential enemies, including humans who come into the gray reef shark's vicinity, are preceded by a complex warning. This includes wagging its head from side to side, sweeping its tail, depressing its pectoral fins, and arching its back. These sharks have severely bitten and injured divers during this threat display.

The gray reef shark is viviparous. Female sharks give birth to up to six pups after a 12-month gestation. Pups are about 20–24 inches (50–60 cm) at birth and reach maturity after about seven years, when they are about 4¼ feet (1.3 m) long.

SNAPSHOT

OTHER NAMES Black-V whaler, longnose blacktail shark
SIZE AT BIRTH 20–24 inches (50–60 cm)
DIET Primarily reef fishes
HABITAT Reef drop-offs and passes, and occasionally on the reef top
DISTRIBUTION Tropical Indo-Pacific, from Hawaii westward

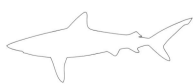

SIZE COMPARISON
Male and female 6 feet (1.8 m)

Lemon Shark

Negaprion brevirostris

Maximum length: 11 feet (3.4 m)

■ MAIN FEATURES

This large, stout-bodied reef shark has a pale yellow-brown body with no obvious markings and a broad, flattened head. It is easily identified by its large dorsal fins, which are about equal in size. The anal fin, immediately below the second dorsal fin, is also large. The pectoral fins are long, and curve back on the trailing edge. There is no lateral keel, and, unlike many other requiem sharks, it has no interdorsal ridge.

The only other species in the genus is the sicklefin lemon shark *Negaprion acutidens*, found in the Indo-Pacific. The trailing edges of its pectoral fins are more curved than the lemon shark's.

The lemon shark is found in tropical reef systems, and is especially abundant in those with sea grass and associated mangrove habitats. It has adapted to be highly tolerant of shallow waters with low oxygen levels, such as warm-water mangrove swamps or bays, places where it is commonly observed. It has attacked humans but is generally not considered aggressive, unless provoked.

Lemon sharks are active throughout the day and night. Among the Bimini Islands population, in the Bahamas,

RESEARCH SUBJECT
A great deal of research has been carried out on the lemon shark because it survives well in captivity.

e level of activity seems to
ncrease at dusk and dawn,
ossibly due to feeding.

FEEDING AND BREEDING
he diet consists of bony fishes,
ays, crustaceans, guitarfishes,
nd mollusks. Some populations
robably undertake lengthy
easonal migrations in search of
od, because they are found in
ummer along sandy beaches and
ontinental shelves in waters of
igh latitudes.

Females reach maturity when
hey are about 8 feet (2.4 m) long,
nd mate in spring and summer.
etween 4 and 17 live young,
bout 2 feet (60 cm) in length, are
orn after a 12-month gestation.

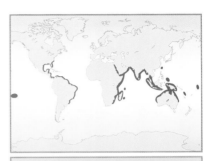

SNAPSHOT

OTHER NAMES **None**
SIZE AT BIRTH **2 feet (60 cm)**
DIET **Bony fish, rays, guitarfish,
crustaceans, and mollusks**
HABITAT **Shallow sea grass beds
and mangrove flats**
DISTRIBUTION **Northeast and
west coasts of Australia,
throughout Southeast Asia,
along the east coast of Africa,
and in the Atlantic off the coasts
of North and South America**

SIZE COMPARISON
■ Male 8½ feet (2.6 m)
☐ Female 8¼ feet (2.5 m)

Leopard Shark

Triakis semifasciata

Maximum length: 7 feet (2.1 m)

■ MAIN FEATURES

Leopard sharks (family Triakidae) are regular and conspicuous inhabitants of most bays along the coast of northern California, USA.

The shark has oval eyes with nictitating membranes. Its two dorsal fins are of similar size, and it has pointed pectoral fins, an anal fin that is smaller than the second dorsal fin, and an asymmetrical caudal fin. Leopard sharks have attractive and elongated bodies, with a series of black spots and saddle-shaped markings on a generally gray background. This makes them popular occupants of public aquariums. They do not need to swim in order to breathe and are usually quite sluggish.

Each year, leopard sharks migrate from the inner bays to the outer coast of the temperate Pacific Northwest. Divers and kayakers will see them there, above the sandy or muddy bottoms of bays and along the outer coast. They are harmless to humans. Because they are social and travel in schools, they are often caught in large numbers.

MISTAKEN IDENTITY
Harmless to humans, the leopard shark is often mistaken for the dangerous tiger shark.

FEEDING AND BREEDING

Leopard sharks have small, pointed teeth, which they use to capture a wide variety of food, including fish, fish eggs, shrimp, crabs, and clams.

At maturity, males are smaller than females, but they ultimately grow to be slightly larger. Females produce up to 24 young in spring.

The species is ovoviviparous, without a yolk-sac placenta. In spring, the females give birth in coastal bays to between 4 and 29 pups per litter, after a gestation period of 12 months.

SNAPSHOT

OTHER NAMES **None**
SIZE AT BIRTH **8 inches (20 cm)**
DIET **Bony fishes, fish eggs, and crustaceans**
HABITAT **Shallow bays and shallow open coastal waters**
DISTRIBUTION **Oregon to Baja California**

SIZE COMPARISON
■ Male 5 feet (1.5 m)
☐ Female 4 feet (1.2 m)

Oceanic Whitetip Shark

Carcharhinus longimanus

Maximum length: 13 feet (4 m)

■ MAIN FEATURES
This requiem shark should not be confused with the more slender, sluggish, and small-finned whitetip reef shark. The oceanic whitetip's enlarged first dorsal fin and long, paddle-shaped pectoral fins are unmistakable. These fins have conspicuous, mottled, white tips; the fins of juveniles may also have black markings.

The oceanic whitetip is a large and stocky gray species, usually found far offshore, from the surface to depths of at least 500 feet (150 m). It prefers the open ocean, and can sometimes be seen from boats or encountered by divers in open water. Although it is generally slow moving, it is dangerous because it has powerful jaws, large teeth, and it will not hesitate to approach swimmers or small boats. It is probably responsible for many of the open-ocean attacks on people after air or sea disasters. It is most abundant in the tropics, but can also be found from coastal California, USA, to southern Australia, following the warm water masses.

SURPRISE BURSTS
The oceanic whitetip is dangerous to humans. Although it is usually a slow swimmer, it can swim quickly in short bursts.

FEEDING AND BREEDING
Oceanic whitetips eat just about anything that they can catch in the open sea, including a variety of fishes and squid, whale carcasses, turtles, sea birds, and garbage disposed of at sea. They are aggressive and will dominate other shark species that are competing for food.

The litter size increases with the size of the mother—as many as 15 live pups are born after a gestation period of 12 months.

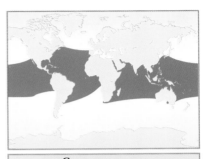

SNAPSHOT

OTHER NAMES Whitetip whaler, whitetip shark
SIZE AT BIRTH 2½ feet (75 cm)
DIET Wide-ranging, including fishes, squid, birds, turtles, and carrion
HABITAT Offshore, from the surface to 500 feet (150 m)
DISTRIBUTION All tropical and subtropical seas

SIZE COMPARISON
■ Male 7½ feet (2.3 m)
☐ Female 7 feet (2.1 m)

Scalloped Hammerhead

Sphyrna lewini

Maximum length: 10 feet (3 m)

■ MAIN FEATURES

Scalloped hammerheads belong to a family of eight sharks with a unique specialization—the front of the skull expands laterally like a hammer to form a head structure called a cephalofoil. This serves many biological functions. Its wide, flattened shape adds lift during swimming, improving hydrodynamic efficiency. The increased surface area allows for the expansion of many sensory systems important for feeding. The eyes are at the tips of the head; the electro-receptors and lateral line are over a wider area. Thus these fast active requiem sharks can capture large or elusive prey.

Scalloped hammerheads can be distinguished by the broad leading edge on the head, which is arched toward the back. There is a prominent indentation in the center with two smaller lobes on either side, giving a scalloped look.

These sharks are found in most warm temperate and tropical waters. They occur in coastal areas above continental

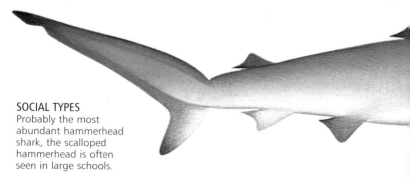

SOCIAL TYPES
Probably the most abundant hammerhead shark, the scalloped hammerhead is often seen in large schools.

island shelves, and in adjacent offshore waters to depths of some 900 feet (270 m).

FEEDING AND BREEDING
Scalloped hammerheads enter shallow bays and estuaries, and aggregate around seamounts. Divers see them interacting, chasing, thrusting, shaking their heads, and biting each other. This behavior needs further study, but may be for social reasons or reproduction. They are often indifferent to divers, but do make close passes.

Their diet consists of bony fishes and cephalopods. Females bear 15 to 30 pups, 17–22 inches (43–55 cm) long at birth.

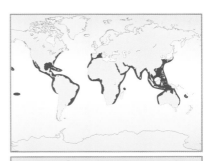

SNAPSHOT

OTHER NAMES **Kidney-headed shark, bronze hammerhead**
SIZE AT BIRTH **17–22 inches (43–55 cm)**
DIET **Bony fishes and squid**
HABITAT **Coastal, from the surface to 900 feet (270 m)**
DISTRIBUTION **Worldwide in tropical and warm-temperate seas**

SIZE COMPARISON
■ Male 8½ feet (2.6 m)
☐ Female 7 feet (2.1 m)

Silvertip Shark

Carcharhinus albimarginatus

Maximum length: 10 feet (3 m)

■ MAIN FEATURES
Silvertips are fairly large and stocky sharks, bronze in color. Their common name is derived from the distinctive white tips and margins on all their fins. The pectoral fins are narrow and pointed, and the first dorsal fin is narrowly rounded. Apart from these features, they look like many of the other requiem sharks that are commonly found out beyond the reef edge in warm, tropical waters.

These sharks prefer offshore islands, coral reefs, and banks. However, they also enter lagoons where they can be encountered often. Given their size and their aggressive behavior, they should always be treated with caution. They have been known to harass divers, but reports of them actually attacking people are rare.

■ FEEDING AND BREEDING
The teeth of silvertips are similar to those of other species that belong to the genus Carcharhinus. They are strongly serrated and narrowly pointed in the lower jaw, and sharp, serrated, and oblique in the upper jaw.

AGGRESSIVE NATURE
The silvertip shark is potentially dangerous and divers should be extremely cautious.

hey are ideal for catching and
utting the fish that they feed
pon, such as reef wrasses and, in
pen water, tuna and flyingfish.

Experiments conducted using
nderwater sound have shown
at silvertips are attracted to
w-frequency sounds, probably
ecause these frequencies mimic
e sound made by an injured
sh, potentially an easy meal.

Silvertip sharks are viviparous;
males usually have 5 or 6 pups
a litter, but there can be as
any as 11. The young hatch
ter 12 months' gestation.

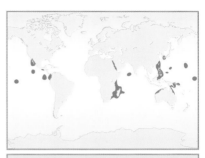

SNAPSHOT

OTHER NAMES **Silvertip whaler**
SIZE AT BIRTH **2⅛ feet (65 cm)**
DIET **Pelagic and bottom fishes**
HABITAT **Along reef drop-offs from
the surface to 2,625 feet (800 m)**
DISTRIBUTION **Widespread in
tropical Indo-Pacific; east coast of
Africa from the Red Sea and South
Africa eastward to the eastern
Pacific and Mexico to Colombia**

SIZE COMPARISON
Male and female 10 feet (3 m)

Swellshark

Cephaloscyllium ventriosum

Maximum length: 3½ feet (1 m)

■ MAIN FEATURES
The swellshark (family Scyliorhinidae) is distinctive, with a broadly rounded snout and small dorsal fins on the rear half of the body, and is covered in large, spiky denticles.

The female swellshark lays large, greenish-amber, purse-shaped eggs among seaweeds. After seven to ten months, depending on the temperature of the water, the unhatched juveniles use their large dermal denticles to pry free of the egg case.

■ PROTECTIVE FEATURES
The shark's patterning of dark brown blotches and saddle-like patterns on the yellow to brown background of its back, along with small, dark spots on its belly and flanks, provides good camouflage for this sedentary shark. It has a wide, grinning mouth laden with small, pointy teeth—very effective for capturing fish that swim by.

Divers, too, frequently overlook swellsharks because of their camouflage. You will see them from 30 feet (10 m) to more than 200 feet (60 m) if you look

SWOLLEN STOMACH
To protect against predators, the swellshark wedges itself between rocks by swallowing large amounts of water to inflate its stomach up to three times its normal size.

...refully in caves and among ...allow rocks and crevices ...round kelp forests. They are ...ot dangerous sharks, unless ...ey are handled and provoked.

As their name suggests, ...wellsharks swell up when they ...e threatened or in any way ...istressed. This is a protective ...echanism. They position ...emselves in a rock crevice or ...her narrow hiding place, and ...ke in large amounts of water to ...alloon themselves. Eventually ...ey are so tightly wedged that ...redators cannot remove them.

SIZE COMPARISON
Male and female 2¾ feet (83 cm)

Tiger Shark

Galeocerdo cuvier

Maximum length: 24 feet (7.3 m)

■ MAIN FEATURES
This large, dangerous shark is to tropical waters what the great white shark is to temperate waters. It is named for the dark stripes on its gray back, which are pronounced in juveniles but become pale or disappear in large adults. Its wide mouth, broad nose, barrel chest, and the slenderness at the base of its tail are distinctive. So, too, are its heavily serrated, cockscomb-shaped teeth. These, combined with its jaw strength, allow it to cut through the bodies of large sea turtles, as well as seals, sea lions, and whales. It also has a liking for venomous jellyfish, stingrays, and sea snakes. One of the few true shark scavengers, this shark has eaten cattle, pigs, donkeys, sheep, and humans that have fallen overboard.

■ FEEDING AND BREEDING
Adult tiger sharks spend their days beyond the reef edge to depths of about 500 feet (150 m), except at certain times of the year when they also come inshore during the day. They are active at night, and enter shallow reefs and lagoons after

NOCTURNAL DANGER
Believed to be nocturnal, the tiger shark is extremely dangerous. It has attacked and consumed swimmers in all seas.

ısk to feed. In certain areas, ıey migrate between island ʲoups to take advantage of ɔlonies of young birds learning fly over water.

 Generally, tiger sharks are ʲuggish, but they can move ıickly when feeding, and should treated with great caution on ɛ rare occasions they are ıcountered. It is best to calmly ɐve the water, keeping the shark sight at all times.

 The tiger shark is the only ʲoviviparous requiem shark. l other requiem sharks are viparous. It has between 10 ıd 82 pups after a 12–month ɛstation period. Tiger sharks ɐture after 4 to 6 years, and live r about 12 years.

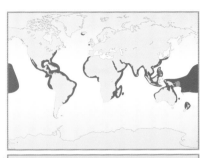

SIZE COMPARISON
■ Male 12 feet (3.7 m)
☐ Female 10 feet (3 m)

Tope Shark

Galeorhinus galeus

Maximum length: 6½ feet (2 m)

■ MAIN FEATURES
The tope shark (family Triakidae) is also known as the soupfin shark. It is a moderately slender shark, bronzy gray on the upper side and pale underneath. It has an unusually large subterminal lobe on the caudal fin. The small second dorsal fin is about the same size as the anal fin.

The tope shark is usually found on continental shelves and continental slopes in temperate waters. It feeds mainly on fish, squid, and octopus near the seabed or in the water column. Often preferring to congregate in schools, it can live to more than 50 years of age.

It is a very shy creature and encounters are unlikely. It will flee long before a diver arrives in its vicinity, though large number of newborn pups are sometimes caught inshore by anglers.

■ BREEDING
Tope sharks migrate long distances so that pregnant female can give birth in cooler waters. Sharks tagged in England and Ireland have traveled to Iceland (1,530 miles [2,460 km]) and the Canary Islands (1,570 miles [2,525 km]). Sharks from the Californian

COMMERCIAL PRODUCT
The flesh, fins, and liver of this shark are much sought after for human consumption.

region have been recaptured off British Columbia (1,000 miles [1,610 km] away).

This shark is ovoviviparous. Litter sizes vary—a litter of 52 pups is the largest known. The pups are born after a gestation of 12 months and they are 12–14 inches (30–35 cm) in length. Discrete, inshore nursery areas have been found in South Africa, Australia, New Zealand, Argentina, and the west coast of North America.

Female sharks reach maturity at eight to ten years and breed only every second or third year. This low reproductive rate, combined with the tope's longevity, has made it vulnerable to overfishing.

SNAPSHOT

OTHER NAMES Soupfin, school, vitamin, and snapper shark
SIZE AT BIRTH 12–14 inches (30–35 cm)
DIET Mostly bony fishes, but also squid and octopus
HABITAT Coastal, from shallow water to 1,800 feet (550 m)
DISTRIBUTION Widespread in Pacific and Atlantic oceans, Mediterranean Sea, southern Australia, and New Zealand

SIZE COMPARISON
■ Male 5¼ feet (1.6 m)
☐ Female 5 feet (1.5 m)

Whitetip Reef Shark

Triaenodon obesus

Maximum length: 7 feet (2.1 m)

■ MAIN FEATURES

The whitetip reef shark should not be confused with the larger and more graceful oceanic whitetip shark. It is a sluggish, fairly slender, gray requiem shark with conspicuous white tips on its dorsal and caudal fins.

It has medium-sized, pointed teeth with smooth edges, which are flanked by small cusps. Whitetip reef sharks live close to shore, at depths of 26–130 feet (8–40 m). During the day, divers and snorkelers predictably find them resting in caves, particularly in Hawaii and the Galápagos Islands, or under rock and coral ledges. They are active at night and during slack tides. They can become accustomed to the sound of boats and to spearfishers, but are aroused by the presence of divers, and will approach them out of curiosity. Although this is not an aggressive species, divers have lost a hand when attempting to feed them.

■ FEEDING AND BREEDING

Unlike most requiem sharks, the whitetip is not an effective fish hunter in open water. It feeds

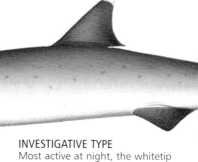

INVESTIGATIVE TYPE
Most active at night, the whitetip reef shark is extremely curious.

mostly on the bottom, taking advantage of its tooth structure and its short, broad snout to pursue prey into reef crevices, where they cannot escape. Like most reef sharks, it too falls prey to other, larger sharks and large reef groupers.

The flesh and liver of whitetips are consumed by humans. It is unique among sharks in having caused ciguateratoxin poisoning, a type of food poisoning with severe gastrointestinal and neurological symptoms.

Whitetip sharks are viviparous. They bear litters of between one and five pups which are born after a gestation period of at least five months.

SNAPSHOT

OTHER NAMES Blunthead shark
SIZE AT BIRTH 21–24 inches
(52–60 cm)
DIET Bottom fishes, crustaceans, and cephalopods
HABITAT A shallow-water reef dweller, to depths of 130 feet (40 m)
DISTRIBUTION Tropical eastern Pacific to eastern Africa, widespread in Oceania

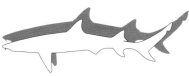

SIZE COMPARISON
■ Male 4½ feet (1.4 m)
□ Female 4¼ feet (1.3 m)

CLASSIFICATION TABLE

ORDER HEXANCHIFORMES
SIXGILL, SEVENGILL, AND FRILLED SHARKS

Family Chlamydoselachidae—
Frilled Sharks

CHLAMYDOSELACHUS ANGUINEUS   Frilled shark

Family Hexanchidae—
Sixgill and Sevengill Sharks

HEPTRANCHIAS PERLO   Sharpnose sevengill shark

HEXANCHUS GRISEUS   Bluntnose sixgill shark

HEXANCHUS NAKAMURAI   Bigeye sixgill shark

NOTORYNCHUS CEPEDIANUS   Broadnose or spotted sevengill shark

ORDER SQUALIFORMES
DOGFISH SHARKS

Family Echinorhinidae—Bramble Sharks

ECHINORHINUS BRUCUS   Bramble shark

ECHINORHINUS COOKEI   Prickly shark

Family Squalidae—Dogfish Sharks

CIRRHIGALEUS ASPER   Roughskin spurdog

CIRRHIGALEUS BARBIFER   Mandarin dogfish

SQUALUS ACANTHIAS   Piked dogfish

SQUALUS BLAINVILLEI   Longnose spurdog

SQUALUS BREVIROSTRIS   Japanese shortnose spurdog

SQUALUS FCUBENSIS   Cuban dogfish

SQUALUS JAPONICUS   Japanese spurd

SQUALUS MEGALOPS   Shortnose spur

SQUALUS MELANURUS   Blacktail spur

SQUALUS MITSUKURII   Shortspine spurd

SQUALUS RANCURELI   Cyrano spurd

Family Centrophoridae—
Gulper Dogfish

CENTROPHORUS ACUS   Needle dogf

CENTROPHORUS ATROMARGINATUS   Black gulper dogfi

CENTROPHORUS GRANULOSUS   Gulper dogf

CENTROPHORUS HARRISSONI   Dumb gulp dogfi

CENTROPHORUS ISODON   Dark gulper dogfi

CENTROPHORUS LUSITANICUS   Lowfin gulp dogfi

CENTROPHORUS MOLUCCENSIS   Smallfin gulp dogfi

CENTROPHORUS NIAUKANG   Taiwan or gia gulper dogfi

CENTROPHORUS SQUAMOSUS   Leafscale gulp dogfi

CENTROPHORUS TESSELATUS   Mosaic gulp dogfi

DEANIA CALCEA   Birdbeak dogfi

DEANIA HYSTRICOSUM   Rough longnose dogfi

DEANIA PROFUNDORUM   Arrowhead dogfi

DEANIA QUADRISPINOSUM   Longsnout dogfi

Family Etmopteridae—Lanternsharks

ACULEOLA NIGRA	Hooktooth dogfish
CENTROSCYLLIUM EXCELSUM	Highfin dogfish
CENTROSCYLLIUM FABRICII	Black dogfish
CENTROSCYLLIUM GRANULATUM	Granular dogfish
CENTROSCYLLIUM KAMOHARAI	Bareskin dogfish
CENTROSCYLLIUM NIGRUM	Combtooth dogfish
CENTROSCYLLIUM ORNATUM	Ornate dogfish
CENTROSCYLLIUM RITTERI	Whitefin dogfish
ETMOPTERUS BAXTERI	New Zealand lanternshark
ETMOPTERUS BIGELOWI	Blurred smooth lanternshark
ETMOPTERUS BRACHYURUS	Shorttail lanternshark
ETMOPTERUS BULLISI	Lined lanternshark
ETMOPTERUS CARTERI	Cylindrical lanternshark
ETMOPTERUS COMPAGNOI	Brown lanternshark
ETMOPTERUS DECACUSPIDATUS	Combtooth lanternshark
ETMOPTERUS GRACILISPINIS	Broadband lanternshark
ETMOPTERUS GRANULOSUS	Southern lanternshark
ETMOPTERUS HILLIANUS	Caribbean lanternshark
ETMOPTERUS LITVINOVI	Smalleye lanternshark
ETMOPTERUS LUCIFER	Blackbelly lanternshark
ETMOPTERUS MOLLERI	Slendertail lanternshark
ETMOPTERUS PERRYI	Dwarf lanternshark
ETMOPTERUS POLLI	African lanternshark
ETMOPTERUS PRINCEPS	Great lanternshark
ETMOPTERUS PUSILLUS	Smooth lanternshark
ETMOPTERUS PYCNOLEPIS	Densescale lanternshark
ETMOPTERUS SCHULTZI	Fringefin lanternshark
ETMOPTERUS SENTOSUS	Thorny lanternshark
ETMOPTERUS SPINAX	Velvet belly
ETMOPTERUS SPLENDIDUS	Splendid lanternshark
ETMOPTERUS TASMANIENSIS	Tasmanian lanternshark
ETMOPTERUS UNICOLOR	Brown lanternshark
ETMOPTERUS VILLOSUS	Hawaiian lanternshark
ETMOPTERUS VIRENS	Green lanternshark
MIROSCYLLIUM SHEIKOI	Rasptooth dogfish
TRIGONOGNATHUS KABEYAI	Viper dogfish

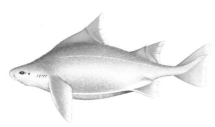

Family Somniosidae—Sleeper Sharks

CENTROSCYMNUS COELOLEPIS	Portuguese dogfish
CENTROSCYMNUS CREPIDATER	Longnose velvet dogfish
CENTROSCYMNUS CRYPTACANTHUS	Shortnose velvet dogfish
CENTROSCYMNUS MACRACANTHUS	Largespine velvet dogfish
CENTROSCYMNUS OWSTONI	Roughskin velvet dogfish
CENTROSCYMNUS PLUNKETI	Plunket shark
SCYMNODALATIAS ALBICAUDA	Whitetail dogfish
SCYMNODALATIAS GARRICKI	Azores dogfish
SCYMNODALATIAS OLIGODON	Sparsetooth dogfish
SCYMNODALATIAS SHERWOODI	Sherwood dogfish
SCYMNODON ICHIHARAI	Japanese velvet dogfish
SCYMNODON RINGENS	Knifetooth dogfish
SCYMNODON SQUAMULOSUS	Velvet dogfish
SOMNIOSUS MICROCEPHALUS	Greenland sleeper shark
SOMNIOSUS PACIFICUS	Pacific sleeper shark
SOMNIOSUS ROSTRATUS	Little sleeper shark

Family Oxynotidae—Roughshark

OXYNOTUS BRUNIENSIS	Prickly dog
OXYNOTUS CARIBBAEUS	Caribbean roughs
OXYNOTUS CENTRINA	Angular roughs
OXYNOTUS JAPONICUS	Japanese roughs
OXYNOTUS PARADOXUS	Sailfin roughs

Family Dalatiidae—Kitefin Shark

DALATIAS LICHA	Kitefin s
EUPROTOMICROIDES ZANTEDESCHIA	Taillight s
EUPROTOMICRUS BISPINATUS	Pygmy s
HETEROSCYMNOIDES MARLEYI	Longnose py s
ISISTIUS BRASILIENSIS	Cookiecutte cigar s
ISISTIUS LABIALIS	China Sea cookiecu s
ISISTIUS PLUTODUS	Largetooth cookiecu s
MOLLISQUAMA PARINI	Softskin dog
SQUALIOLUS ALIAE	Smalleye pygmy s
SQUALIOLUS LATICAUDUS	Spined pygmy s

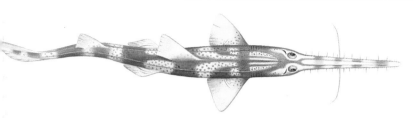

ORDER PRISTIOPHORIFORMES
SAWSHARKS

Family Pristiophoridae—Sawsharks

PLIOTREMA WARRENI   Sixgill sawshark

PRISTIOPHORUS CIRRATUS   Common sawshark

PRISTIOPHORUS JAPONICUS   Japanese sawshark

PRISTIOPHORUS NUDIPINNIS   Shortnose sawshark

PRISTIOPHORUS SCHROEDERI   Bahamas sawshark

ORDER SQUATINIFORMES
ANGELSHARKS

Family Squatinidae—Angelsharks

SQUATINA ACULEATA   Sawback angelshark

SQUATINA AFRICANA   African angelshark

SQUATINA ARGENTINA   Argentine angelshark

SQUATINA AUSTRALIS   Australian angelshark

SQUATINA CALIFORNICA   Pacific angelshark

SQUATINA DUMERIL   Sand devil

SQUATINA FORMOSA   Taiwan angelshark

SQUATINA GUGGENHEIM   Angular angelshark

SQUATINA JAPONICA   Japanese angelshark

SQUATINA NEBULOSA   Clouded angelshark

SQUATINA OCCULTA   Hidden angelshark

SQUATINA OCULATA   Smoothback angelshark

SQUATINA SQUATINA   Angelshark

SQUATINA TERGOCELLATA   Ornate angelshark

SQUATINA TERGOCELLATOIDES   Ocellated angelshark

ORDER HETERODONTIFORMES
BULLHEAD SHARKS

Family Heterodontidae—Bullhead Sharks

HETERODONTUS FRANCISCI   Hornshark

HETERODONTUS GALEATUS   Crested bullhead shark

HETERODONTUS JAPONICUS   Japanese bullhead shark

HETERODONTUS MEXICANUS   Mexican hornshark

HETERODONTUS PORTUSJACKSONI   Port Jackson shark

HETERODONTUS QUOYI   Galápagos bullhead shark

HETERODONTUS RAMALHEIRA   Whitespotted bullhead shark

HETERODONTUS ZEBRA   Zebra bullhead shark

ORDER ORECTOLOBIFORMES CARPETSHARKS

Family Parascylliidae—Collared Carpetsharks

CIRRHOSCYLLIUM EXPOLITUM — Barbelthroat carpetshark

CIRRHOSCYLLIUM FORMOSANUM — Taiwan saddled carpetshark

CIRRHOSCYLLIUM JAPONICUM — Saddled carpetshark

PARASCYLLIUM COLLARE — Collared carpetshark

PARASCYLLIUM FERRUGINEUM — Rusty carpetshark

PARASCYLLIUM VARIOLATUM — Necklace carpetshark

Family Brachaeluridae—Blind Sharks

BRACHAELURUS WADDI — Blind shark

HETEROSCYLLIUM COLCLOUGHI — Bluegray carpetshark

Family Orectolobidae—Wobbegongs

EUCROSSORHINUS DASYPOGON — Tasselled wobbegong

ORECTOLOBUS JAPONICUS — Japanese wobbegong

ORECTOLOBUS MACULATUS — Spotted wobbegong

ORECTOLOBUS ORNATUS — Ornate wobbegong

ORECTOLOBUS WARDI — Northern wobbegong

SUTORECTUS TENTACULATUS — Cobbler wobbegong

Family Hemiscylliidae—Longtailed Carpetsharks

CHILOSCYLLIUM ARABICUM — Arabian carpetsh

CHILOSCYLLIUM BURMENSIS — Burm bamboosh

CHILOSCYLLIUM GRISEUM — Gray bamboosh

CHILOSCYLLIUM HASSELTI — Indones bamboosh

CHILOSCYLLIUM INDICUM — Slender bamboosh

CHILOSCYLLIUM PLAGIOSUM — Whitespo bamboosh

CHILOSCYLLIUM PUNCTATUM — Brownban bamboosh

HEMISCYLLIUM FREYCINETI — Indonesian speck carpetsh

HEMISCYLLIUM HALLSTROMI — Papuan epaul sh

HEMISCYLLIUM OCELLATUM — Epaulette sh

HEMISCYLLIUM STRAHANI — Hooded carpetsh

HEMISCYLLIUM TRISPECULARE — Speck carpetsh

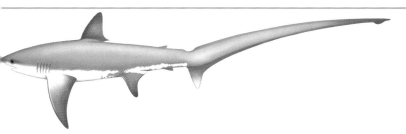

Family Ginglymostomatidae— Nurse Sharks

JDOGINGLYMOSTOMA BREVICAUDATUM
    Shorttail nurse shark

GLYMOSTOMA CIRRATUM   Nurse shark

RIUS FERRUGINEUS   Tawny nurse or giant sleepy shark

mily Stegostomatidae—Zebra Sharks

GOSTOMA FASCIATUM   Zebra shark

mily Rhincodontidae—Whale Sharks

NCODON TYPUS   Whale shark

ORDER LAMNIFORMES MACKEREL SHARKS

Family Odontaspididae— Sand Tiger Sharks

CHARIAS TAURUS   Sand tiger, spotted raggedtooth, or gray nurse shark

CHARIAS TRICUSPIDATUS   Indian sand tiger

ONTASPIS FEROX   Smalltooth sand tiger or bumpytail raggedtooth

ONTASPIS NORONHAI   Bigeye sand tiger

Family Pseudocarchariidae— Crocodile Sharks

PSEUDOCARCHARIAS KAMOHARAI   Crocodile shark

Family Mitsukurinidae—Goblin Sharks

MITSUKURINA OWSTONI   Goblin shark

Family Megachasmidae— Megamouth Sharks

MEGACHASMA PELAGIOS   Megamouth shark

Family Alopiidae—Thresher Sharks

ALOPIAS PELAGICUS   Pelagic thresher

ALOPIAS SUPERCILIOSUS   Bigeye thresher

ALOPIAS VULPINUS   Thresher shark

Family Cetorhinidae—Basking Sharks

CETORHINUS MAXIMUS   Basking shark

Family Lamnidae—Mackerel Sharks

CARCHARODON CARCHARIAS   Great white shark

ISURUS OXYRINCHUS   Shortfin mako

ISURUS PAUCUS   Longfin mako

LAMNA DITROPIS   Salmon shark

LAMNA NASUS   Porbeagle shark

ORDER CARCHARHINIFORMES
GROUND SHARKS

Family Scyliorhinidae—Catsharks

APRISTURUS ACANUTUS	Flatnose catshark
APRISTURUS ATLANTICUS	Atlantic ghost catshark
APRISTURUS BRUNNEUS	Brown catshark
APRISTURUS CANUTUS	Hoary catshark
APRISTURUS FEDOROVI	Federovís catshark
APRISTURUS GIBBOSUS	Humpback catshark
APRISTURUS HERKLOTSI	Longfin catshark
APRISTURUS INDICUS	Smallbelly catshark
APRISTURUS INVESTIGATORIS	Broadnose catshark
APRISTURUS JAPONICUS	Japanese catshark
APRISTURUS KAMPAE	Longnose catshark
APRISTURUS LAURUSSONI	Iceland catshark
APRISTURUS LONGICEPHALUS	Longhead catshark
APRISTURUS MACRORHYNCHUS	Flathead catshark
APRISTURUS MACROSTOMUS	Broadmouth catshark
APRISTURUS MADERENSIS	Madeira catshark
APRISTURUS MANIS	Ghost catsh
APRISTURUS MICROPS	Smalleye catsh
APRISTURUS MICROPTERYGEUS	Smalldo catsh
APRISTURUS NASUTUS	Largenose catsh
APRISTURUS PARVIPINNIS	Smallfin catsh
APRISTURUS PINGUIS	Fat catsh
APRISTURUS PLATYRHYNCHUS	Spatulasn catsh
APRISTURUS PROFUNDORUM	Deepwater catsh
APRISTURUS RIVERI	Broadgill catsh
APRISTURUS SALDANHA	Saldanha catsh
APRISTURUS SIBOGAE	Pale catsh
APRISTURUS SINENSIS	South China catsh
APRISTURUS SPONGICEPS	Spongehead catsh
APRISTURUS STENSENI	Panama ghost catsh
APRISTURUS VERWEYI	Borneo catsh
ASYMBOLUS ANALIS	Gray spotted catsh
ASYMBOLUS VINCENTI	Gulf catsh
ATELOMYCTERUS FASCIATUS	Banded sand catsh
ATELOMYCTERUS MACLEAYI	Australian mar catsh

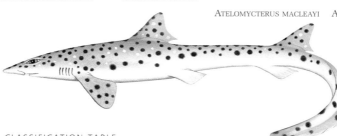

...OMYCTERUS MARMORATUS	Coral catshark	GALEUS EASTMANI	Gecko catshark
...OHALAELURUS KANAKORUM	New Caledonia catshark	GALEUS GRACILIS	Slender sawtail catshark
...OHALAELURUS LABIOSUS	Blackspotted catshark	GALEUS LONGIROSTRIS	Longnose sawtail catshark
...HAELURUS ALCOCKI	Arabian catshark	GALEUS MELASTOMUS	Blackmouth catshark
...HAELURUS CANESCENS	Dusky catshark	GALEUS MURINUS	Mouse catshark
...HAELURUS CLEVAI	Broadhead catshark	GALEUS NIPPONENSIS	Broadfin sawtail catshark
...HAELURUS DAWSONI	New Zealand catshark	GALEUS PIPERATUS	Peppered catshark
...HAELURUS HISPIDUS	Bristly catshark	GALEUS POLLI	African sawtail catshark
...HAELURUS IMMACULATUS	Spotless catshark	GALEUS SAUTERI	Blacktip sawtail catshark
...HAELURUS LUTARIUS	Mud catshark	GALEUS SCHULTZI	Dwarf sawtail catshark
...ALOSCYLLIUM FASCIATUM	Reticulated swellshark	GALEUS SPRINGERI	Springer's catshark
...ALOSCYLLIUM ISABELLUM	Draughtsboard shark	HALAELURUS BOESEMANI	Speckled catshark
...ALOSCYLLIUM LATICEPS	Australian swellshark	HALAELURUS BUERGERI	Blackspotted catshark
...ALOSCYLLIUM SILASI	Indian swellshark	HALAELURUS LINEATUS	Lined catshark
...ALOSCYLLIUM SUFFLANS	Balloon shark	HALAELURUS NATALENSIS	Tiger catshark
...ALOSCYLLIUM UMBRATILE	Japanese swellshark	HALAELURUS QUAGGA	Quagga catshark
...ALOSCYLLIUM VENTRIOSUM	Swellshark	HAPLOBLEPHARUS EDWARDSII	Puffadder shyshark
...ALURUS CEPHALUS	Lollipop catshark	HAPLOBLEPHARUS FUSCUS	Brown shyshark
...US ARAE	Roughtail catshark	HAPLOBLEPHARUS PICTUS	Dark shyshark
...US ATLANTICUS	Atlantic sawtail catshark	HOLOHALAELURUS PUNCTATUS	African spotted catshark
...US BOARDMANI	Australian sawtail catshark	HOLOHALAELURUS REGANI	Izak catshark
		PARMATURUS CAMPECHIENSIS	Campeche catshark
		PARMATURUS MACMILLANI	New Zealand filetail
		PARMATURUS MELANOBRANCHIUS	Blackgill catshark

PARMATURUS PILOSUS	Salamander shark
PARMATURUS XANIURUS	Filetail catshark
PENTANCHUS PROFUNDICOLUS	Onefin catshark
PORODERMA AFRICANUM	Striped catshark or pyjama shark
PORODERMA PANTHERINUM	Leopard catshark
SCHROEDERICHTHYS BIVIUS	Narrowmouth catshark
SCHROEDERICHTHYS CHILENSIS	Redspotted catshark
SCHROEDERICHTHYS MACULATUS	Narrowtail catshark
SCHROEDERICHTHYS TENUIS	Slender catshark
SCYLIORHINUS BESNARDI	Polkadot catshark
SCYLIORHINUS BOA	Boa catshark
SCYLIORHINUS CANICULA	Smallspotted catshark
SCYLIORHINUS CAPENSIS	Yellowspotted catshark
SCYLIORHINUS CERVIGONI	West African catshark
SCYLIORHINUS COMOROENSIS	Comoro catshark
SCYLIORHINUS GARMANI	Brownspotted catshark
SCYLIORHINUS HAECKELII	Freckled catshark
SCYLIORHINUS HESPERIUS	Whitesaddled catshark
SCYLIORHINUS MEADI	Blotched catshark
SCYLIORHINUS RETIFER	Chain catshark
SCYLIORHINUS STELLARIS	Nursehound
SCYLIORHINUS TOKUBEE	Izu catshark
SCYLIORHINUS TORAZAME	Cloudy catshark
SCYLIORHINUS TORREI	Dwarf catshark

Family Proscylliidae—Finback Catsh

CTENACIS FEHLMANNI	Harlequin cats
ERIDACNIS BARBOURI	Cuban ribbontail cats
ERIDACNIS RADCLIFFEI	Pygmy ribbontail cats
ERIDACNIS SINUANS	African ribbontail cats
PROSCYLLIUM HABERERI	Graceful cats

Family Pseudotriakidae— False Catsharks

| GOLLUM ATTENUATUS | Slender smoothhc |
| PSEUDOTRIAKIS MICRODON | False cats |

Family Leptochariidae— Barbeled Houndsharks

| LEPTOCHARIAS SMITHII | Barbeled hounds |

Family Triakidae—Houndsharks

FURGALEUS MACKI	Whiskery s
GALEORHINUS GALEUS	Tope shark, sou school shark, or vitamin s
GOGOLIA FILEWOODI	Sailback hounds
HEMITRIAKIS ABDITA	Deepwater sick hounds
HEMITRIAKIS JAPANICA	Japanese topes
HEMITRIAKIS FALCATA	Sicklefin hounds
HEMITRIAKIS LEUCOPERIPTERA	Whitefin topes
HYPOGALEUS HYUGAENSIS	Blacktip topes
IAGO GARRICKI	Longnose hounds
IAGO OMANENSIS	Bigeye hounds

USTELUS ANTARCTICUS	Gummy shark	MUSTELUS PUNCTULATUS	Blackspot smoothhound

USTELUS ANTARCTICUS — Gummy shark

USTELUS ASTERIAS — Starry smoothhound

USTELUS CALIFORNICUS — Gray smoothhound

USTELUS CANIS — Dusky smoothhound

USTELUS DORSALIS — Sharpnose smoothhound

USTELUS FASCIATUS — Striped smoothhound

USTELUS GRISEUS — Spotless smoothhound

USTELUS HENLEI — Brown smoothhound

USTELUS HIGMANI — Smalleye smoothhound

USTELUS LENTICULATUS — Rig or spotted estuary smoothhound

USTELUS LUNULATUS — Sicklefin smoothhound

USTELUS MANAZO — Starspotted smoothhound

USTELUS MENTO — Speckled smoothhound

USTELUS MINICANIS — Dwarf smoothhound

USTELUS MOSIS — Arabian, hardnose, or Moses smoothhound

STELUS MUSTELUS — Smoothhound

STELUS NORRISI — Narrowfin or Florida smoothhound

STELUS PALUMBES — Whitespot smoothhound

MUSTELUS PUNCTULATUS — Blackspot smoothhound

MUSTELUS SCHMITTI — Narrownose smoothhound

MUSTELUS SINUSMEXICANUS — Gulf smoothhound

MUSTELUS WHITNEYI — Humpback smoothhound

SCYLLIOGALEUS QUECKETTI — Flapnose houndshark

TRIAKIS ACUTIPINNA — Sharpfin houndshark

TRIAKIS MACULATA — Spotted houndshark

TRIAKIS MEGALOPTERUS — Spotted gully shark or sharptooth houndshark

TRIAKIS SCYLLIUM — Banded houndshark

TRIAKIS SEMIFASCIATA — Leopard shark

Family Hemigaleidae—Weasel Sharks

CHAENOGALEUS MACROSTOMA — Hooktooth shark

HEMIGALEUS MICROSTOMA — Sicklefin weasel shark

HEMIPRISTIS ELONGATUS — Snaggletooth shark

PARAGALEUS LEUCOLOMATUS — Whitetip weasel shark

PARAGALEUS PECTORALIS — Atlantic weasel shark

PARAGALEUS RANDALLI — Slender weasel shark

PARAGALEUS TENGI — Straighttooth weasel shark

Family Carcharhinidae—
Requiem Sharks

CARCHARHINUS ACRONOTUS	Blacknose shark
CARCHARHINUS ALBIMARGINATUS	Silvertip shark
CARCHARHINUS ALTIMUS	Bignose shark
CARCHARHINUS AMBLYRHYNCHOIDES	Graceful shark
CARCHARHINUS AMBLYRHYNCHOS	Gray reef shark
CARCHARHINUS AMBOINENSIS	Pigeye or Java shark
CARCHARHINUS BORNEENSIS	Borneo shark
CARCHARHINUS BRACHYURUS	Bronze whaler or copper shark
CARCHARHINUS BREVIPINNA	Spinner shark
CARCHARHINUS CAUTUS	Nervous shark
CARCHARHINUS DUSSUMIERI	Whitecheek shark
CARCHARHINUS FALCIFORMIS	Silky shark
CARCHARHINUS FITZROYENSIS	Creek whaler
CARCHARHINUS GALAPAGENSIS	Galápagos shark
CARCHARHINUS HEMIODON	Pondicherry shark
CARCHARHINUS ISODON	Finetooth shark
CARCHARHINUS LEIODON	Smoothtooth blacktip
CARCHARHINUS LEUCAS	Bull or Zambezi s[hark]
CARCHARHINUS LIMBATUS	Blacktip s[hark]
CARCHARHINUS LONGIMANUS	Oceanic whit[e] s[hark]
CARCHARHINUS MACLOTI	Hardnose s[hark]
CARCHARHINUS MELANOPTERUS	Blacktip reef s[hark]
CARCHARHINUS OBSCURUS	Dusky s[hark]
CARCHARHINUS PEREZI	Caribbean reef s[hark]
CARCHARHINUS PLUMBEUS	Sandbar s[hark]
CARCHARHINUS POROSUS	Smalltail s[hark]
CARCHARHINUS SEALEI	Blackspot s[hark]
CARCHARHINUS SIGNATUS	Night s[hark]
CARCHARHINUS SORRAH	Spottail s[hark]
CARCHARHINUS TILSTONI	Australian black[tip] s[hark]
CARCHARHINUS WHEELERI	Blacktail reef s[hark]
GALEOCERDO CUVIER	Tiger s[hark]
GLYPHIS GANGETICUS	Ganges s[hark]
GLYPHIS GLYPHIS	Speartooth s[hark]
ISOGOMPHODON OXYRHYNCHUS	Daggernose s[hark]

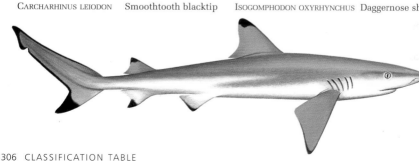

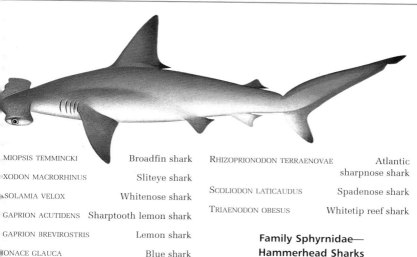

MIOPSIS TEMMINCKI	Broadfin shark	
XODON MACRORHINUS	Sliteye shark	
SOLAMIA VELOX	Whitenose shark	
GAPRION ACUTIDENS	Sharptooth lemon shark	
GAPRION BREVIROSTRIS	Lemon shark	
ONACE GLAUCA	Blue shark	
IZOPRIONODON ACUTUS	Milk shark	
IZOPRIONODON LALANDEI	Brazilian sharpnose shark	
ZOPRIONODON LONGURIO	Pacific sharpnose shark	
ZOPRIONODON OLIGOLINX	Gray sharpnose shark	
ZOPRIONODON POROSUS	Caribbean sharpnose shark	
ZOPRIONODON TAYLORI	Australian sharpnose shark	

RHIZOPRIONODON TERRAENOVAE	Atlantic sharpnose shark
SCOLIODON LATICAUDUS	Spadenose shark
TRIAENODON OBESUS	Whitetip reef shark

Family Sphyrnidae— Hammerhead Sharks

EUSPHYRA BLOCHII	Winghead shark
SPHYRNA CORONA	Mallethead shark
SPHYRNA LEWINI	Scalloped hammerhead
SPHYRNA MEDIA	Scoophead shark
SPHYRNA MOKARRAN	Great hammerhead
SPHYRNA TIBURO	Bonnethead shark
SPHYRNA TUDES	Smalleye hammerhead
SPHYRNA ZYGAENA	Smooth hammerhead

GLOSSARY

Agonistic Aggressive or combative; usually in reference to behavior.

Barbels Slender, fleshy protuberances, usually near the nostrils, that have a sensory function, the exact nature of which is unknown.

Benthic Bottom dwelling.

Bioluminescence The production of light by living organisms; common in deep-water sharks.

By-catch Fishes caught incidentally by fishing operations that are targeting other species.

Caudal keel A fleshy ridge running along the base of a shark's tail.

Cephalopods A class of mollusks, including squid and octopus.

Chemosensory Having a sensory sensitivity to chemicals.

Chum Collective term for the various baits—including fish oil and mammal blood—used to attract and feed sharks.

Claspers The external male reproductive organs of sharks.

Cloaca Combined reproductive and excretory cavity.

Crustaceans Creatures with horny exoskeletons, including barnacles, krill, copepods, crabs, shrimps, and prawns.

Denticles The toothlike scales attached to a shark's skin.

Dentition The type and arrangement of teeth.

Dermis The inner layer of a shark's skin, comprising cells in a network of tissue fibers.

Ecology The science that focuses on the relationship between organisms and their environment.

Elasmobranch The group of cartilaginous fishes comprising the sharks and rays.

Endothermic Internally warmed.

Epidermis The outer layer of a shark's skin, composed of multiple layers of cells.

Epipelagic Inhabiting the upper levels of the ocean.

Finning The practice of cutting the fins off sharks, sometimes while they are still alive.

Gill filaments Thin, platelike structures, rich with blood vessels, that allow the exchange of oxygenated water and waste during respiration.

Gillnets Underwater fishing nets used to enmesh sharks and other fishes by their head and gills, or body and fins.

Gill rakers Specialized, toothlike structures inside the gill slits for straining particles from the water.

Gill slits The external openings of the gill system.

Intertidal Describing the area that falls between the limits of low and high tide.

Intra-uterine oophagy The reproductive process in which embryos feed from unfertilized eggs during gestation.

Invertebrates All animals without backbones.

Labial furrows Grooves around the mouths of some sharks.

Lateral line A system of paired sensory tubes, running beneath a shark's skin from the head to the base of the caudal fin, that is involved in the detection of vibrations in the water.

Longlines Underwater fishing lines with a long main line that has numerous, equally spaced short lines attached, each baited with a hook.

Meshing Setting large, wide-meshed gillnets parallel to beaches to catch sharks in order to reduce the risk to humans.

Neuromasts Sensory cells with hairlike protrusions, which are sensitive to vibrations in the water.

Nictitating membrane A tough inner eyelid that protects the eyes of certain sharks when feeding.

Ovoviviparity The most common form of shark reproduction, whereby the egg is encased until the embryo is fully formed, but remains inside the shark's body; also known as aplacental viviparity.

Pelagic Swimming freely in the open ocean; not associated with the bottom.

Pericardial cavity The body cavity that contains the heart.

Pharynx The mouth cavity.

Photophores Luminous organs on deep-water fishes.

Pit organs Small, blind pockets in the skin, containing hair cells, which are sensitive to vibrations in the water. Pit organs, which are protected by pairs of denticles, are associated with, but not connected to, the lateral line.

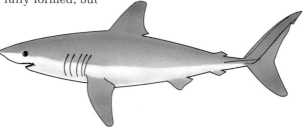

Placental viviparity The form of shark reproduction whereby uncased embryos remain inside the mother until birth, during which time they are sustained by way of a placenta.

Placoid Platelike; used in reference to a shark's dermal denticles.

Plankton Minute animals or plants that drift in the open sea. Animal plankton is known as zooplankton; plant plankton is known as phytoplankton.

Precaudal pit A notch just in front of the caudal fin.

Spiracle An auxiliary respiratory opening behind the eyes.

Subterminal notch An indentation along the lower margin of the upper lobe of the caudal fin.

Suctorial Adapted for sucking.

Symbiosis Any close relationship between two organisms that is beneficial to at least one of them.

Top predator An animal that is at the top of the food chain and is usually not preyed upon by any other animal.

Tricuspid Having three cusps; used in reference to teeth.

Vertebrates All animals that have a backbone, or spinal column.

Visceral cavity The trunk cavity containing internal organs.

Viviparity Reproduction whereby young develop inside the mother's body; also known as placental viviparity.

INDEX

Page numbers in *italics* indicate illustrations and photos

ACKNOWLEDGMENTS

[t = top, b = bottom, l = left, r = right, c = center, F = Front, C = Cover, B = Back]

Picture Credits

Ad-Libitum/Stuart Bowey 145t. **Kelvin Aitken** 25t, 45t, 171t. **Auscape** 99t, 147r (Doug Perrine); 146b (Graham Robertson). **Australian Picture Library** 155t, 155b (Attila A. Bicskos); 149t (Greenpeace/Grace); 77b (Lightstorm); 79t, 94b (Pacific Stock); 57c (Volvox/Marine); 82b, 144b (ZEFA); 69c, 128r. **Corel** 12, 36, 41, 51t, 58c, 59c, 83c, 104c, 142c, 143c, 152c, 160b, 161b, 168c, 169c, 182c, 190c, 208c, 216c, 232c. **Digital Stock** 10–11c, 12c, 13c, 15t, 22b, 23t, 29t, 34b, 35t, 36c, 37c, 67c, 84c, 85c, 87c, 88b, 89b, 92b, 93t, 95b, 101t, 101b, 102–103c, 104c, 105c, 107t, 109c, 110b, 111t, 113b, 117t, 119t, 121r, 132b, 142c, 151b, 152c, 153c, 154b, 156b, 158b, 159b, 163c, 164–165c, 168c, 216c, 232c. **Getty Images/Image Bank** 106bl. **Nature Travel and Marine Images** 99b (Cherie Vasas). **C. S. Johnson** 120t, 121t. **Ocean Earth Images** 71t (Michael Cufer); 170b (Barbara Evans); 56b, 65t, 95t, 118b, 120b, 148b, 157t, 157b, 158t (Kevin Deacon). **Photo Disc** 108r. **Photo Essentials** 84c. **photolibrary.com** 68t (Michael Aw); 150b (Simon Fraser/SPL); 127b (IBA Collection). **Terry Walker** 25b. **Weldon Owen** 171r.

Illustration Credits

Martin Camm 20, 21, 27, 31, 70, 76, 97, 114, 115. **Greg Campbell** 139, 141. **Christer Eriksson** 86. **Chris Forsey** 18, 19, 44, 100. **Peg Gerrity** 63. **Ray Grinaway** 30, 32, 40, 43, 46, 47, 52, 53, 54, 61, 74, 75, 90, 91, 112, 116, 130, 131, 136, 137, 138, 140, 141, 147, 165, 173, 174, 176, 177, 178, 180, 182, 183, 184, 186, 188, 190, 191, 192, 194, 196, 198, 200, 202, 204, 206, 209, 210, 212, 214, 217, 218, 220, 222, 224, 226, 228, 230, 233, 234, 236, 238, 240, 242, 244, 246, 248, 250, 254, 256, 258, 260, 262, 264, 266, 268, 270, 272, 274, 276, 278, 280, 282, 284, 286, 288, 290, 294, 297, 298, 299, 301, 302, 305, 306, 307. **Gino Hasler** 38, 60, 63, 64, 68, 69, 70, 72, 73, 78, 96, 98, 144. **David Kirshner** 14, 15, 16, 17, 24, 28, 55, 73, 82. **Frank Knight** 26, 27, 97. **Alex Lavroff** 141. **Colin Newman/Bernard Thornton Artists UK** 26, 27. **Tony Pyrzakowski** 50, 53, 112, 122, 123, 136, 137, 138, 139, 140, 141, 145, 292, 300, 309, 310, 311. **Trevor Ruth** 88. **Michael Saunders** 27. Peter Schouten 27. **Stephen Seymour/ Bernard Thornton Artists UK** 151. **Roger Swainston** 22, 33, 35, 43, 48, 49, 54, 68, 74, 76, 77, 80, 81, 82, 208. **Rod Westblade** 114.

The publishers would like to thank the following people for their assistance in the preparation of this book: Sarah Anderson, Kate Brady, Megan Wardle (editorial assistance); Puddingburn Publishing Services (indexing).

Consultant Biography

Consultant Editor **Terence I. Walker** is the Program Leader, Modelling and Data Management, and heads a program of study of sharks at the Marine and Freshwater Resources Institute in Victoria, Australia. He has more than 30 years' experience in shark fisheries stock assessment, research, and management. He has published more than 100 scientific papers and management reports.